Other books by Monika Hellwig:

What Are the Theologians Saying?
The Meaning of the Sacraments
The Christian Creeds

MONIKA HELLWIG
TRADITION
THE CATHOLIC STORY TODAY

Pflaum Publishing Dayton, Ohio 45439

CONTENT

FOR MARIANNE
AND
DAVID JOHN
WHO KNOW IT ALL ANYWAY
FROM EXPERIENCE

INTRODUCTION:
SEVERAL QUESTIONS

There are at present so many urgent and anxious questions within the Catholic community concerning religious education; one book cannot possibly address itself to all of them. This book is concerned with a contemporary appraisal of our Catholic heritage, with an attempt to describe coherently what it is that we have to pass on to newcomers and to future generations. Thus there is a whole range of questions concerning those to whom this heritage is offered that this book does not attempt to discuss at all—most importantly the question concerning the age at which ritual and community experiences and explanations might be offered and the many questions concerning mode and techniques of communication. There are many good books on these topics, but they frequently are read by persons whose fundamental anxiety is that they really do not understand what it is they are supposed to be passing on in their teaching and catechetical activities.

Concerning the scope—or what we usually have called the

content of Catholic religious education—we appear to be in a rather serious crisis of understanding and of confidence. Religious education, or catechesis, is simply the formalized process of tradition, the "handing on" of the Christian experience with its rituals, goals and ideals, and explanations. What we are speaking of then as "content" of the tradition basically is a way of life and a set of convictions.

There are many reasons why we should be in crisis today over this handing-on process. First, we have realized particularly sharply that a way of life and a set of convictions are not passed on by words alone, much less by formal classroom presentation alone. Yet most of us who are now parents or catechists look back to our own religious education to discern in it the unquestioned assumption that words carried the whole message, though reinforced by example and disciplinary measures. It is clear now that the type of formal religious education we received often missed the point because it put the cart before the horse, though we did receive some authentic Christian education more or less by accident. The conclusion too often drawn from this observation today is that the cart is unnecessary really, and it could best be used to build a glorious bonfire. But the fact remains that the horse alone cannot carry very much.

We once memorized a catechism that contained in brief and enigmatic formulations the outcome of lengthy, intricate, and sometimes rather abstract or rather specialized arguments in the history of the Church community. Beginning from such formulations, we would be led into explanations intended to make them clear to us and to point out their relevance to our living of Christian lives. Careful scrutiny of some of these catechisms today suggests that some questions and answers simply might have been omitted altogether; they no longer were issues. In other words, not every formulation to which the Christian community came with great struggle and anguish need be thought of as integral to an under-

2

standing of the Christian life and vision at all times and in all cultures. Some formulations were local and particular. But who today is to decide which is which?

Moreover, with the knowledge that we have today of ourselves as persons, learners, decison makers, and value shapers, we become aware that the catechisms from which we learned not only contained some quite unnecessary questions (and omitted some crucial ones), but that they were written, so to speak, back-to-front or upside-down. They made a false assumption that Christian life followed when one began with clear and orthodox definitions and explanations. They assumed that the first order of business in the "learning" of Christian life was memorization and repetition of the correct, official explanations that then could be elaborated with practical applications.

We are vividly aware today that formulations arise and come to make sense on the basis of the living experience, not the other way around. Life always structures itself, but structures cannot beget life. The doctrine of the Church is a theory built from the praxis of thoughtfully and reflectively living the Christian life; it is not a preexistent theory from which the life can be derived. It is this reality that gives some of the older catechisms the "back-to-front" appearance.

However, we tend to find ourselves nowadays sliding very quickly at this point from a crisis of understanding into a crisis of confidence.

The crisis of understanding is clear. It prompts the questions: What *is* a "front-to-front" catechesis? Can such a catechesis be set forth formally? Do we always have to wait to respond to people's life-questions as they come, so that when these questions never touch Jesus Christ or the Reign of God or the task of the Church community or its sacramental life or beliefs, these topics do not appear in religious education? But this concern leads to the further question: If what is passed on is only what is asked specifically by the learner, who will be the teacher for the next generation? Does it not mean a constant impoverishment of the tradition, the heritage of the community?

These questions must be asked because the crisis of understanding is becoming a crisis of confidence. In our present anxiety that the enterprise as we have known it might be humanly and practically speaking inauthentic, we may be in danger of not carrying out the task of tradition, of the "handing over" at all. Worse still, if all those who have serious questions as to the authenticity of present or past patterns of religious education in the Catholic community evade the issue of Christian "content," the task of tradition in the community may be left to those who understand it least, who may attribute to the formulations an almost magical power to get the work of the Church community accomplished.

If we ask the question "Can faith be taught, can religion be taught?" the answer, of course, is that they cannot be taught. They are essentially personal responses, deeply rooted in a well-matured freedom of perception, judgment, and decision. But this answer does not exhaust the question. Faith cannot be taught. It can be invited, encouraged, and supported. The Church community as such is the most basic support and invitation. Its legend and folklore, its ritual celebrations, its language of symbols, its code of action are all aspects of support, encouragement, and also of a process of formation of vision, judgment, and decision-making habits. This is why all these aspects play such an important role in the task of tradition, the business of the "handing on" of Christianity. This is why they all constitute part of any formal process of religious education and why they all have a certain inner coherence as a community experience.

Understanding of and familiarity with these various aspects and the experience as a whole are gained basically by participation and by "learning the story." It would seem that, at this time, we rather urgently need to rediscover the Christian experience and its story. For too many contemporary Catholics, participation has been disillusioning and the story has been told without understanding. We still need a constant process of personal breakthrough and rediscovery even by deeply committed Christians and theologically sophisticated Christians before we will have a modest supply of preachers and catechists who can assume the task of handing on the heritage *with confidence.* This book is concerned with this extremely urgent need. It attempts to reconstruct in contemporary terms a sketch for the Christian "story"-that is, an account of the total Christian vision, showing its inner coherence and its strength.

This book is not concerned with devices for attracting absent teenagers back to the churches and to religion classes. It is concerned with what we have to say to those who willingly and questioningly come, even if that were to include only three or four young persons in a parish. It is not concerned with numerical increase of those participating in adult education classes in the parishes. It is concerned with what there is to say to those who do come. Neither is the book concerned with what could and should be said to children at different ages and stages of commitment. It is concerned with discovering a coherent account of ourselves as a believing community, an account that explains it satisfactorily to ourselves and to other interested adults. This view is stated not because I consider it unimportant to hand over the experience of the community to our children and to share with them our convictions, but because I fear that this important enterprise may be entirely worthless if we are not clear ourselves, within an adult frame of reference, about what it is that we are passing on.

CHAPTER 1:
THE BEGINNING IS NOW

The present anxiety over what we should be handing on in the Catholic tradition is an anxiety that we may not be able to give a coherent account of ourselves as a believing community. In other words, it is a fear that we do not ourselves have a coherent understanding of our stance as Catholics—of what really is the core or essence of Catholic tradition.

In one sense, the only thing that is strange about this circumstance is that it troubles us so. We may be in trouble because of a false expectation that persists. There is a tendency to look for the "content" rather than the "scope" of the tradition, the message, the faith. Both words have a range of meaning in ordinary usage, and they need to be defined here. We have spoken often of the content of Catholic belief, or the content of catechetical instruction, meaning a clearly defined list of propositions, or an agreed inventory of information, combined with an explicit and finite code of commands or rules of conduct. "Content" usually has implied an already determined product of a process that has been completed in the past by other people, that we receive intact and pass along intact. "Content" usually has implied, though most of us have not been aware of it explicitly, a certain alienation of ourselves as thinking, problem-solving, world-building, creative persons. The word "content" often has carried the subtle implication that our Catholic tradition and our Catholic life and commitment are given, not made; superimposed, not constructed by us and among us.

In the sense just described, content is what many Catholics of our time are rebelling against in frustration, as persons confronted with questions and problems and challenges that always seem to leap so far beyond the neatly packaged catechesis that was handed down. At the same time, it sometimes seems that few people go beyond this to a constructive consideration of alternative ways of understanding tradition. It is easier simply to reject the particular package that does not fit and to demand another authoritative package in its stead that would fit rather than reflect whether any predetermined package is really the substance of our tradition.

By comparison, "scope" is a word that applies to projects not yet finished, to a course of action that has not been or cannot be predetermined. It applies to a message whose implications are yet to unfold. The scope of Catholic tradition means all those aspects of life and reality with which the tradition is concerned. The scope of Catholic teaching means all those matters to which the teaching addresses itself. The scope of catechesis means all that should be explained, shown, related, offered to newcomers in order that they may have entrance into the life experience of the community of Catholic believers. It means that with which newcomers need to be acquainted. But it is acquaintance with a many-dimensional, living reality that escapes precise definition, that often is open to various interpretations.

To say that we should be looking for scope rather than content is to suggest that we are in the midst of a search. Our commitment is to that search and to the community that is making that search. Not only the catechesis that we offer to newcomers but our own mature, adult, continuing study and preoccupation must be with that search that is still in progress.

Any search, obviously, implies that we have some idea of what it is we are looking for, some idea as to where and how we might expect to find it. But any search also implies that there is something we have not yet found. This would seem to be the proper model for the core and focus of Catholic tradition. The important question that immediately must be asked is: What is it we seek? The answers are so simple that we easily might miss them while looking for something more complicated. What we seek in the Catholic tradition, the Catholic community, the Catholic life is salvation—salvation of each individual and the salvation of the world. The whole endeavor of Catholicism (and of Christianity in all its traditions) makes no sense except in terms of an experienced need of salvation—that is, in the realization from one's experience that things are not as they ought to be in our lives and in the world and that they might be so different. Besides this, Catholicism (and all Christianity) makes no sense at all except to those who have glimpsed a promise or a possibility of making things quite different and for whom this glimpse was one that showed Jesus as Christ present here and now.

When we speak of the content of Christian tradition or of catechesis, there is always the danger that we are not beginning here and now in our own lives and experience with the felt need of salvation; rather we are taking for granted that the logical and psychological order is to begin elsewhere, at another time long ago, among other people, with events we know from hearsay. Then we have the problem of trying to prove that this package of hearsay information from long ago has some relevance now to our lives and hopes and fears. Moreover, questions of what is central and what is peripheral, what adaptations might be made, and so on, become word games of logical calculations or matters of pure opinion. In other words, a notion of tradition that makes it a dead bundle leads sooner or later to confusion and disillusionment and to no real respect for tradition at all.

To some extent, this process seems to have happened to us in the Catholic community today. We took Catholic tradition for something ready-made and finished, as though it had dropped out of heaven at some time in the past, and men had had no role in shaping it. The result in our times has been a degree of disillusionment; many Catholics now observe an embarrassed silence and studied disinterest towards Catholic tradition and the treasures from centuries of Catholic experience. This attitude has led to a succession of crises in catechesis and preaching.

The purpose of this book is to suggest that the scope of Catholic doctrine and wisdom—and therefore the scope of religious education—includes the whole experience and reflection of the community through the ages in all its many expressions. The starting point is indeed now—but in the here and now that is shaped and constituted by our past as a characteristic moment of need and opportunity for the future. So the understanding of Catholicism and of what it is that we as Catholics have to pass on as our tradition, our life and vision and ideals must begin here and now with the need for salvation and the hope for salvation as we experience it. But this expectation, in turn, is constituted already by the cultural and spiritual heritage that shapes our perception and experience, for good and for ill, coherently or with much conflict, serenely or with anger and confusion. Much in our experience of the past and its influence may be negative, but it cannot be ignored because it keeps cropping up again as unfinished agenda. To stand in the present is to reach out to full personal freedom and to the fullest possible possession of our "now" in order to shape our future. We must appropriate in depth the traditions that have shaped us and our community and our situation.

Again, the search must be based on some idea of what we are looking for—salvation known negatively by the need we experience and positively by promissory experiences, glimpses of hope, suggesting what might be and may be. But it also must be based on some idea as to where and how we may find what we are looking for. This is where Catholicism differentiates itself from other strands of Christianity. It has characteristic ways of looking at the community experience through the ages, at what we have handed down across the generations. Regarding the community experience and traditions with the expectation of "content," many of us have become thoroughly disenchanted with Catholicism as a package that always falls short of answering our real questions or even of allowing them as real questions. With the expectations of "content," we often have reduced Catholicism to dogmatic and moral formulations officially endorsed, to canon law, to officially sanctioned liturgical practice, to the governmental and organizational structure of the Church as institution, and to the history of all of these—that history often seen as now more or less complete and as having established a now unchanging pattern.

With the expectations implicit in "scope," Catholicism becomes once again an immensely rich heritage—vast, elusive in its multifaceted complexity, often offering a great range of alternatives, often stimulating hitherto unasked questions, inexhaustible in any one lifetime. It is the concern of this book to suggest avenues of exploration within the scope of Catholicism and of Catholic religious education that seem quite frequently to escape notice. For 20 centuries, a whole people, with varying degrees of commitment and insight, has lived an attempt to respond to the call and vision of Jesus Christ—not only bishops, popes, and religious professionals, but a whole people. And this is a people that has cut across many cultures, languages, nations, economies; a people that includes poets and visionaries, blue-collar and white-collar workers, the simplest and the most educated, scientists and civil servants, men and women. This Christian experience is far broader than the things that have happened in churches and church services or the things that have been done by the clergy.

The characteristically Catholic way of looking at the Christian message and the Christian hope is that all of this matters, that there is something to be learned from it, that we do not always begin at the same point. The beginning is now; but it is always a characteristic and unique now, constituted by all this rich past, every shred of which helps or hinders, every move of which becomes part of the matter for critical reflection as to what we have learned about the Christian quest for salvation. This awareness implies a great respect for tradition, a great respect for what we have received from those who lived before us in this endeavor, a great concern to be at home within the tradition, knowing its experiences and having followed its reflections. But it implies a very active, creative participation in that experience and reflection. It implies that we appropriate it as our own in the process of confronting our own questions and challenges, in the process of trying to understand and interpret our own situation and our own vocation within our world and our time in history.

A difficulty immediately suggests itself. Many, perhaps most, Catholics have not been accustomed to regard their Catholicism in this way. They personally may never have appropriated it. It may have begun in childhood and continued all their lives to be something quite alien to their personal quest for salvation. What they seek and what they question in their lives, what is wrong and what they hope can be changed may all have been experienced and thought through without any reference to a religious faith or their Church membership. It may never have occurred to them to relate it in any way to the promise of redemption by Jesus Christ, and they might find it quite fanciful to apply the word "salvation" to their hopes and dreams. Meanwhile, they have accepted religion as something that is entitled to a sector of their lives. They know it is concerned with the ultimate—ultimate meaning of their lives, ultimate criteria for a good life, ultimate outcome. But this ultimate is often easily interpreted as "beyond death" so that religion becomes something like an insurance payment. Whatever "salvation" may mean in this context, it is not something that arises out of each person's experience and reflection, a felt need, but rather something based on hearsay, something that is known to be needed only on someone else's word and for which there is no meaningful descriptive definition. In other words, this notion of salvation and the observances advertised as a necessary condition for this salvation can only be alienating.

This is a situation with which most of us are all too familiar. The question arises as to how it can be changed, how the focus can be readjusted when the pattern of expectations is already set and often is reinforced heavily by the way parishes and other church structures function. Most difficult of all is the question as to what can be done once we realize how deeply ingrained this false order is in those of us who are leaders and initiators in Church circles—religious educators, clergy, theologians, and, always, of course, at the grass roots, parents. It is clear that this is a delicate task. But it is equally clear from centuries of Christian experience that in all sorts of different circumstances people broke through the barriers of preconceived categories that put religious hopes into an unreal setting. The great innovators—saints, heroes, mystics— have been people who made such radical breakthroughs and personally appropriated the endeavor.

It has always been said that this kind of breakthrough is the fruit of prayer and of continuous renunciations. This is certainly true, but probably only if prayer and renunciation are properly understood. If prayer and renunciation are un-

derstood and practiced as observances precisely of the alienated kind of Church membership described above, they can
only reinforce that alienated pattern. Prayer practiced because one knows by hearsay that one ought to pray—such as
Sunday Mass participation because one has always assumed
it is compulsory and there is no option—is extremely unlikely
to offer any breakthrough points. Renunciation practiced for
its own sake—because one has accepted on hearsay that it is a
good or even necessary practice—offers minimal likelihood of
discovering a new life and new dimensions of life at the price
of that renunciation.

It is clear that prayer has to be in a spirit of search, has to
be a way of tuning in to revelation in Jesus Christ, has to be
in the hope of having one's eyes opened to greater truth, if it
is to be the means of breakthrough to a personal appropriation of one's religious heritage. It is equally clear that it is
not renunciations as such that are helpful in this way, but
only renunciations that really do serve to sharpen or correct
one's personal focus, renunciations that really do set one free
to look at an issue afresh without interference from self-interest. But the question remains as to how this can be done.

In trying to make a breakthrough to a personal and creative appropriation of one's religious heritage, it would seem
that a catalyst is always needed to make it possible to set out
from where one actually is here and now. Sometimes that
catalyst is a tragedy, an unexpected frustration of one's immediate goals, a deeply moving experience of friendship or of
falling in love—an event that reveals a transcendent dimen-
sion of everyday life and prompts the questions. What then is
life and existence really about when it has such depth? What
is the meaning of it all? There is much religious literature that
attempts to trigger this type of response in the reader without
his personally having come to such a crisis point in his life.
Some persons seem to be quite alert and responsive to such

appeals, but most people in our culture leave that sort of thing to poets.

There is another and more laborious way of attempting to trigger a breakthrough that may be more helpful today to most adults in our culture, especially when the effort has to be in terms of groups, perhaps large groups. This is by way of a direct attempt to bring to reflexive awareness people's real though perhaps inchoate sense of the need for salvation. With any group of people really willing to make an attempt to ask more fundamental questions about their own values and motivations, someone with a good sense of the Catholic heritage can easily serve as a catalyst of a process of search and rediscovery and personal appropriation of the religious stance implied in Catholicism, even if he is in doubt as to how far he himself has personally appropriated the heritage with which he is intellectually well acquainted.

The basic questions such a group needs to ask itself are along the following lines. What are our practical concerns at the moment? What absorbs our spare time and our efforts? Options for the children's schooling, or some project for the neighborhood, or the re-carpeting of the house . . .? Why are these things important? What do we hope to achieve by them? Gradually the honest pursuit of these questions by a group of people who trust one another enough to do their thinking out loud leads closer and closer to the questions of what we care about most, what the meaning of life is for us at present, in an operative sense. It is not important what we usually would formally say are our ultimate concerns. It is very important to trace back our immediate concerns to their ultimate sources in our order of values.

At some such stage, another set of questions might be introduced if these questions have not spontaneously arisen in the process of trying to answer the first set. What do we think are the problems in our society, in our neighborhood, in our city? What needs to be changed so that people can live decent lives? What would each of us like to change so as to be perfectly happy? The purpose of discussing questions like these is to uncover each person's felt need for salvation not only for himself but for society, and in the discussion to press some of the unanswered questions.

With a group of people who care about finding religious roots, there will be a spontaneous turning to the religious heritage as a resource. But unless someone is present who is somewhat seriously acquainted with the heritage and can direct the group in a process of new discoveries, such attempts have a disastrous tendency to foreshorten themselves with clichés and misunderstandings. Even if the discussion does not spontaneously turn to the religious heritage as a resource, the competent person functioning as a catalyst can throw in the comments that open up this possibility. "Well, isn't this something that was a major issue for the first Christians?" "This problem has come up before, in a slightly different context. Is it worth our while in this group to find out what happened?" "There are stories in the Bible that seem to be an effort to capture just this sort of question. Would it be helpful for us to read them with some good commentary?"

This kind of discussion can and usually does lead to meditation on the gospel and its implications, to some forms of shared prayer that offer community support to each person in the search. It can and should lead to personal prayer that reaches far beyond where each person now stands. Such discussion also leads inexorably to considerations of what it is that would make our lives more coherent, would put our values into better order, would make our society and our world better. This, in turn, raises the question of hope against cynicism, which is the basic religious question, the question of salvation and of the source from which we expect salvation. To carry on such a consideration seriously over a period of time sooner or later raises the exigence of quite extensive and radical renunciations from the people involved. But this is never renunciation for its own sake; it is simply the process of ruthless selection and elimination of possibilities in life in order to pursue a vision and a hope.

There are of course very many groups doing this kind of thing today, but it seems that they often do not have the benefit of the wisdom of the community with all its long and rich and varied experience. What seems to be needed is a more thoroughly Catholic approach that assumes that there is much to be learned from this intervening experience and much to be gained by a joining of efforts in the search. That is why this book attempts to point out avenues and vistas to be explored as part of the Catholic search.

NOTES

The notion of scope rather than content is discussed at length and very helpfully in *Program Planning for Adult Christian Education* by James R. Schaefer (Newman Press). It was he who persuaded me that it would be very useful to introduce this word to wider circles of Catholics and to keep explaining what is at stake in the idea. His book is to be recommended very strongly for ideas and insights on the implementation of the change of perspective implied in the change of words.

CHAPTER 2:
THE COMMUNITY IS HERE

It has become quite chic to complain that most Catholics have never had any experience of community: The parish is not a community, and thus much of what is being written and discussed about Church as it might be is simply beside the point. This seems a strange argument; yet it is used for writing books and articles about community (which could not possibly help, of course, unless the readers had indeed had an experience of what it is we are discussing).

The simple answer to this objection is that community is where you make it. To be alive as a human individual speaking a language and wearing clothes is to have participated in community. Community is wherever people join their efforts towards a common purpose, wherever people surrender or sacrifice in some measure their individual or partisan interests in order to pursue a common interest. There are, of course, different degrees or levels of intensity in community associations. There are people who live in a neighborhood and therefore become in many ways an interest group. Even if they care little for one another, out of sheer self-interest they will have to join their efforts sometimes towards a common purpose. This is why we refer quite glibly to the Forest Hills community or the River City community. There are people who follow similar money-making occupations and therefore, if only out of sheer self-interest, will pursue some common goals. Thus we commonly speak of the professional community, the academic community, and so on.

But there are ascending levels of intensity of association and of common purpose and endeavor. That is why throughout this book the terms, "the Catholic community," "the community of believers," "the Church community," are used without apology. Each time the term "community" is used, the intensity of association implied has to be inferred from the context. It varies, of course, a great deal. By the very fact that people gather in the church building on Sunday for the celebration of the Eucharist, they are in an acceptable sense a community; they are joining their efforts for a common purpose; they have given up other individual pursuits in order to engage in this common activity. The point is made here not just to quibble about words but to guard against a certain kind of elitism and to point out that the foundations for building a very strong, intense community relationship do not need to be laid afresh; they are already there.

When people complain that their parish is not a community, they may mean any of several quite different criticisms. They may mean that they themselves do not know other families in the parish, and they feel that it would be proper to a parish to have more explicit personal bonds; but it is always up to someone else to do something about it. Or the criticism may be that the clergy do not have a personal relationship to their parishioners; they consider themselves administrators, fund-raisers, and dispensers of ritual grace. Or again, the criticism may be that the parish is so run that it is difficult or impossible for lay people to take any active role in shaping its policies and life. It simply may be that the pastor expects the people to contribute as much money as he determines he needs for "his" plant and projects, but he considers them incompetent to share in the decisions as to what plant and projects should be maintained or initiated.

These are very different kinds of problems. The problems among the lay people of the parish may be a function of the sheer size of the parish or of the cultural patterns of the society in general. In our society people do not necessarily introduce themselves to all the other families in their residential neighborhoods. They tend to associate by name and personally only when there are certain very specific common interests, such as membership in the same PTA or common professional interests. If the parish does not function as such a common interest group, it may be that it is too large, that it cuts across other lines of association, or that it competes in a society where everyone already has far too many obligations of personal relationship. One can only relate personally and in any depth with a few persons. When every organization, institution, business, school, club, and so on tries to draw all members of the family into intense personal involvement whenever one member of the family is employed or enrolled, the whole network of relationships becomes artificial, the exchanges between persons are not stimulating or supportive but exhausting and depressing and crushingly alienating of the person.

Clearly, in such a society, to hope that the parish may engage people in extensive networks of real interpersonal relationships in which each family will know many other families personally is to be very wide of the mark as far as the salvation of alienated persons and structures in Christ is concerned. What people most of all do not need is one more organization pulling their lives and focus and family apart, one more push to make the meaningless merry-go-round go faster, one more compulsory weekly "cocktail party" where people endlessly play their programmed records as they float by one another with the programmed smile and the programmed glass (coffee cup) in hand, to do their weekly programmed "relating."

In a society such as we have, we all desperately need to be redeemed from inauthentic relationships, inauthentic roles we insistently are called upon to play, inauthentic "communities" into which we are swept. A major reason for the lack of personal focus and for the justified sense of deep alienation from our true selves is surely the vast number of contrived and superimposed "communities" into which we are co-opted. We are urged to play roles that do not ring true, that possibly fulfill no particular purpose, that burden us with exhaustion and depression. The presently quite fashionable call for more community in the parish may be much in danger of missing what salvation in Jesus Christ is. It is always a temptation in professionals of any sort to see the world as entirely organized around their specialty. The dentist talks about diet as though a child were composed entirely of teeth. The IRS expects us to keep financial records as though that were our principal hobby all year rather than a desperate ordeal for several nights in early spring. One could give several books full of examples.

In our Catholic parishes, we have lived through an era of culture change where the Church is not the focus of all social life as it sometimes has been in peasant and immigrant communities. In this change, it certainly has been a temptation of the parish clergy to try to maintain the world they knew and in which they were at home by having all kinds of activities to which people were supposed to come on weekday nights, from potluck suppers to the sodalities and the altar and rosary society, not to mention bazaars to raise money for the school and such. The problem now may be that the enthusiastic lay people who are emerging as parish leaders, whether they are directors of religious education or members of the liturgy committee or social justice committee or parish council, may simply be pushing the same reactionary trend further by calls for "community" that are not too well thought out in terms of the gospel of Jesus Christ.

One does not produce a community by organizing it from above. Where there is a community, it will organize itself; but community grows at the grass roots. To bring it about by a coup d'état so that the whole congregation now sings a particular kind of music, or comes up to stand around the altar, or responds in programmed chorus to the lector's "Good morning" is not to foster community but only to alienate people further. To pressure or shame everybody into participating in parish projects—sociable, charitable, or pious—has the same effect. The fact that the leadership that is applying the pressure now frequently is lay does not change the human effect (and therefore the effect that the action has in terms of salvation). The problem here is that people are coming to church with certain reasons and certain expectations and a certain existing sense of belongingness and community; it is not possible simply to take advantage of their being there to co-opt them into a quite different style of association designed by a few leaders and imposed on the whole parish, thereby to produce "community" at a deeper level of involvement or intensity than formerly existed. But it may produce greater alienation and frustration.

Yet there obviously is a stubborn element of truth in the widespread complaint about lack of community in parishes. It may emerge most clearly in the relation between clergy and laity and in particular between pastor and laity. Usually, upon careful questioning, challenging, and further reflection, the complaint is reduced to the observation that the typical lay person's experience in the parish is still one of passivity and domination. He finds that he is being told what he thinks and feels and what his desires and anxieties are; he is being given the answers to the questions he "ought" to be asking;

he is informed why he is a Catholic and why he comes to church on Sundays. Certain questions and problems are eliminated as questions he must not or simply does not have. He is being told what it means for him to be a follower of Jesus Christ as though that had all been predetermined and blueprinted long ago, and his life could just be a xerox copy.

People are protesting precisely that they expect the Church to be quite different from many of the other associations into which they find themselves co–opted. They are aware, though they may not have articulated it explicitly, that salvation involves the overcoming of the alienation of self. It involves the reclaiming of personal authenticity by accepting personal responsibility for the focus of one's life. They are aware that this must mean asking the ultimate questions for oneself and struggling for answers that are not ready-made. They are aware also that this requires common endeavor, association, and exchange with others; but this association has to be as between equals in the quest. There always can be more mature wisdom in some than in others. There certainly can be expertise gained by academic study of particular questions or simply by wider experience or better access to information. But there cannot be some people taking over the responsibility for questioning or deciding from others and exercising it for them.

The distinctions here are quite subtle, and that means that leadership within the Church is a sacred and delicate trust, just as much when exercised by lay persons as when exercised by clerics. The access leaders have within Catholic circles to an existing community, a "captive" congregation in the parishes, constitutes a danger and a temptation against the gospel as well as an opportunity to strive to realize the gospel. The Catholic parish has certain characteristic problems and opportunities because of the traditional Catholic understanding of the Church as community.

Sociologists some generations ago pointed out that there

are two basic and rather different configurations of community—the one that is taken for granted, and the one that is contracted. The original German words sometimes have been translated "community" and "society." The traditional Catholic emphasis, both in our practice and in our ecclesiologies, has focused heavily on the first, whereas Protestant churches in the West, because of their particular history, have had to emphasize the latter.

The Catholic understanding of the Church as community has supposed that membership comes as part of, but much more than, the cultural heritage. This supposition implies that one comes in adulthood to a personal appropriation of what was in childhood pure gift, but gift of a sort that has been constitutive of one's person.

The Catholic, in other words, is envisaged as coming to recognize himself as he truly is, experiencing his basic orientation as authentic and strong, and affirming it in an act of profound inner freedom. If this is to be possible, several conditions must be verified. First, it cannot possibly be genuine unless each person is given the social and psychological freedom to opt out as well as in when he comes to a critical point of personal decision. Second, if it is genuine, then people will come to such critical points of decision according to unique personal timetables. Some will recognize one dramatic moment, some will be conscious only of a gradually emerging personal conviction and stance, and some will fail to mature to the point of really making a personal decision. In other words, this model of Church community can function authentically only if its community activities allow for the participation of people at all stages of maturity and of individuals along the whole range of possible unique life experiences and timetables. This, however, is an almost impossible challenge.

We are sufficiently aware today that because of the massive civil power the Church has wielded in the past, and because of constant human failure of officials within the Church structures to respect the human dignity and freedom of others, and because of the constant human tendency to evade radical questions of personal stance and conviction, we have had and do have a Catholic membership that, as far as can be judged from action, has not in large numbers come to a personal, free appropriation of the gift of the tradition. It also has become painfully clear that after many generations of this circumstance, catechesis, theology, preaching, sacramental practice, Church structure, and Catholic life have taken on a pattern that is clearly geared to those who have not personally and freely appropriated their heritage. Much on the Catholic scene still supposes that Catholics live with a "consummated freedom," consummated by someone else on their behalf at some inaccessible point in the past.

This, of course, is a parody of the way the believer is understood in traditional Catholic ecclesiology, and the treason involved is clear. What may not be clear is the opposite danger and the reason for it. The opposite danger is the "new Protestantism." The classic protest for which Protestantism is named is basically the protest on behalf of mature, personal faith as the touchstone of salvation rather than ritual involvement. Protestants, however, nevertheless formed churches, and they counted in their membership families faithful over many generations; they taught Bible and Christianity to their children, attempting to pass along the heritage from generation to generation. There have been groups that would baptize only adults, and groups who excluded from membership those who did not give evidence of personal and mature faith. Most of these groups have had to modify their understanding and their practice. There seems to be a danger today that enthusiastic lay leadership in Catholic circles may espouse extreme forms of the Protestant models of Church community without having understood their implications and limitations.

24

Protestant practice and theory indeed have concentrated on the understanding of the churches as contract communities. But it has been acknowledged, for instance, in the American expression "WASP" that the reality may be much closer to the other model, an identification that in the first place is a gift embedded in the person's cultural heritage and that can only be truly a faith when he comes to a critical point of mature personal decision, which for a particular individual may or may not ever happen. Nevertheless, the ease with which Protestants in fact contract in and out of local churches of various denominations means that the Protestant pastoral situation is quite different from the Catholic one. It may be modish for Catholic leadership to demand in Catholic parishes the kind of personal relationships among the members that often are observed in small Protestant congregations, but there is the danger of bringing about a state of affairs that would be far more inauthentic than anything that we have seen so far.

In terms of parish congregations, the only honest approach to community is to acknowledge that the expectation that is traditional—and still that of most parish-loyal Catholics—is that of the community that is taken for granted. And the bond of that community is the common heritage that is a gift from the past; it has to be respected precisely as common heritage and as gift of the whole community. The expression of that community is most obviously and universally the willingness to hold Eucharist together in the parish church on Sunday, or at least to participate on occasion. This is community, and it is genuine, though it still may fall far short of a personal decision of faith in Jesus Christ. What can best be done to foster this community toward the kind of relationships that best allow individuals to make a radical personal decision is to bring the common heritage to reflexive awareness and adult consideration.

This opportunity, again, can be offered but not forced.

Within Catholic practice, the large community that is taken for granted always has been balanced by small contract communities that do not substitute for but supplement the individual's basic membership. Prayer groups, Bible study groups, and action groups follow in this pattern. In them, the more intense level of interpersonal relationship is rightly expected to occur; they are small, they are chosen carefully, and they are authentically contract groups. Thus, the individual person normally should not be alienated or dominated within them, but rather he should find in them the kind of interaction that helps him towards a clearer personal focus of his life. It often is in such groups that Church as community grows at the grass roots. In them, people make a personal appropriation of their Catholic stance and thereby become active members able to turn to the clergy and scholars as resource persons without surrendering their personal responsibility for the Christian search. The remainder of this book is concerned with indicating the resources that we have for the search in our Catholic heritage.

NOTES

The idea of *Gemeinschaft* and *Gesellschaft* (community and society, or the community that is taken for granted and the community that is contracted) is that of Ferdinand Tönnies.

The best book on the Christian understanding of community (or brotherhood) probably is *The Open Circle,* by Josef Ratzinger (Sheed & Ward).

CHAPTER 3:
A HISTORY OF HOPE AND HEROES

If Christianity is hard to explain, this is at least in part because it is not first and foremost a belief system that has been passed on and is being passed on. Rather, it is a visionary hope. All religion is concerned with the reconciliation of man to God. But this concern can be considered in two ways. It might mean a reconciling of each man's consciousness to what is, cultivation of an attitude of resignation to or acceptance of the way things are. This consciousness would require the elaboration of a belief system that justifies, by superhuman sanctions, the way things now are. It would require an ethic that is mainly an ethic of acquiescence and unquestioning obedience. It would hold out rewards to those who acquiesce, who make no waves in the stream of human history.

But reconciliation of man to God can be understood in another way. It can be viewed as the reconciling of what is in fact going on in the world with what ought to be. It requires more than the changing of each man's inner consciousness; it calls for a change in the world, in the structures of human society, in the use of power and the access to material resources. It demands the transformation of human history. This mode of reconciliation requires an ethic, therefore, not of obedience, in the usual sense of the word, but rather of openness to the self-revelation of God in human history and openness to great possibilities of going beyond all the limits of selfishness, suspicion of the unknown, greed, partisan interests, competitiveness, need for self-assertion, prejudices, and so forth. It holds out rewards to those who are generous, who take great personal risks in order to make this a better world.

The question with which Christianity begins is: What is there to hope for in the future of mankind? If we have difficulty in attaining a coherent understanding of our Catholic heritage today, that may be in part because we have been—as a Church community—quite ambiguous about the question and very ambivalent about the answer. As the Catholic heritage was passed on to most of us in this generation, the question concerning the hope for mankind was set aside quietly while emphasis was placed on what each man might hope to attain after death. Thus many of us grew up with an instinctive aversion to involvement in public responsibility, feeling at best that it was time wasted and at worst that one was getting deep into the mud of something dirty by its very nature. It probably is not too strong to say that most of us who are Catholics today were raised with a profound, if unnamed and unrecognized, pessimism about the future of human history and the possibility of changing the injustices of the world in relation to war, poverty, crime, fear, and the human degradation of the powerless of the world. That, after all, was the wicked world, and heaven would duly compensate those who suffered without resentment and those who were compassionate towards the suffering.

Here clearly is one of those cases in which not to decide is to decide. Not to ask the question clearly, persistently, exigently is to make quite unwarranted assumptions about the answer. I believe that we now are tripping and stumbling on those unwarranted assumptions, and we can begin to get ourselves and our account of ourselves together again only by asking that first question quite honestly. As Christians, we ask the question concerning the hope for the future of mankind within a very specific frame of reference. Because we claim to be followers of Jesus, we ask first what is the hope of Jesus for the future of mankind; because we claim to know Jesus as mediated to us by those who witnessed the Resurrection, we ask more specifically what is the hope of the community that rallied in the name of the Risen Christ.

That early community of the followers of Jesus, in assembling the gospels from the existing lore about Jesus—and in choosing that these four and no others were the official accounts of the gospel (good news) of the Lord Jesus Christ— gave us an early record of what was the hope that Jesus held out to them. The gospels portray Jesus constantly proclaiming the nearness of the Reign of God (or Kingdom of Heaven). Nowhere do they define what is meant by the term "Reign of God." They did not need to define it because it was an important term in the religious convictions and expectations of Israel. The idea was not new in the teaching of Jesus. What was new was the insistence, the urgency, with which he announced that the Kingdom of God was within reach. Most of the passages in the gospels beginning "The Kingdom of Heaven is like . . ." are not concerned really with what it is like at all but with how it may be expected to come and with what is the appropriate way of life on our part to bring about the Reign of God.

To understand what is the hope of Christians, then, it is necessary to ask what was the expectation of the Reign of God among Jews of the time of Jesus. They spoke of the kingship or reign of "the heavens" as a circumlocution for "God." Israel had a personal name for the one, transcendent God: Yahweh. But it was avoided in speech as a mark of special reverence. Instead, terms such as "my Lord" and "heaven" and "the heavens" were used. In the term "Kingdom of Heaven," as used at that time by Jews, including Jesus, there was no implication whatever that the Kingship of God in its fullness—the fulfillment of God's promises—would take place somewhere other than in the world we know or in a different time sequence than the history we know. That was not the meaning of "heaven" (literally "the skies") in this expression. Heaven or the Kingdom of God is contrasted to our lives in history as we are leading them now, as the goal is set over against the process or way to the goal.

In presenting this contrast between what is now and the goal towards which we so urgently are invited, the New Testament uses the term "world" in a way that may be confusing to the modern reader. "World," in the whole Bible, very seldom means the cosmos or natural universe. It most frequently means that "world of affairs" that is man-made, including all structures of government, language and communication, laws and customs and cultures, economy, patterns of education, role expectations, the values and priorities by which people make their decisions and shape their own lives and those of others. When the world is presented in the Bible as wicked and in opposition to God or to the Reign of God, the sense is that of a critique of the values and priorities by which the structures of society are set up and decisions are made.

The contrast in the Hebrew Scriptures is not between Israel and the world that is opposed to God but between the world of affairs as it now is and the Reign of God that is to come when the world shall have been transformed. Israel, ideally, is God's witness people; it anticipates the Reign of God in the life and values and priorities of its own people. In practice, Israel is far from this; it comes under constant criticism of its prophets. In the New Testament, the contrast is not between the Church and the world that is opposed to God but between the Reign of God and that world. Ideally, the community—the assembly or Church of the followers of Jesus—is God's witness people; it anticipates the Reign of God by the values and priorities by which it shapes its life as a community in a world that does not function by those values. In practice, it is far from this; it has in the past and must still come under the constant criticism of its own prophets.

In the first place, therefore, the hope of the Reign of God, the hope of heaven, is not concerned with a promise of ultimate human happiness in union with God *to be attained when one can withdraw from the world of human affairs;* it is concerned with a promise of ultimate human happiness in union with God *to be attained when this world shall have been transformed in accord with God's call to men.* That view raises two questions. One has to do with the hope for each individual person because generation after generation dies within a world of human affairs that is unjust, oppressive, and cruel to minorities, to the weak, to the dependent. And some who so die have sacrificed themselves with utmost generosity for the life and happiness of others.

This question, of course, always has troubled sincere believers. If God is just and all-powerful and has revealed to mankind how we should live, then it is always a scandal, a stumbling block, that those who live generously and relate honestly and truthfully to others should be taken advantage of and suffer for it and that God does not, in fact, intervene to rescue them. Prayerful and saintly people reflected on this long before the time of Jesus. One thing was clear to all: God is faithful; he is to be trusted even though those faithful to him die apparently abandoned. God is not outdone in fidelity, and those who spend themselves to bring about his kingship in the world of men surely are not deprived of their own personal, ultimate fulfillment and happiness. How this can come about, we do not know; but we have total faith in God. If one takes this position, by implication one also maintains

31

that personal fulfillment for the individual is possible not only at the attainment of the goal but also in the process of striving for it.

At the time of Jesus, this much was agreed on among Jews because it was the minimum assumption that could be made about a just God who was all-powerful and cared as a Father about each human person whom he summoned into existence. However, in response to repeated wonderings as to how this could be so, a very poetic explanation became current and popular. When that great day comes, it was said, God will awake from the sleep of death and raise from their graves all those who have died seeking to bring closer the Reign of God among men.

In the New Testament, we meet this concept as the position of the Pharisees, those who cherish the whole tradition of Israel whether or not particular details can be documented from the canon of Scripture. The Sadducees attacked it as a pious, perhaps frivolous, accretion to what God had really revealed. The New Testament shows us Jesus and Paul explicitly aligning themselves with the Pharisees on this issue, though neither is willing to venture a description of such a risen life other than that it is quite different from anything that can be imagined and is not to be thought of simply as a continuation of our present life. Jesus Christ, as presented to us in the gospels, is concerned to preserve the mystery, to emphasize the need for real trust in God, and yet to offer a bright, positive description of the hope held out to the individual, such as could capture the imagination of even the least-educated people.

The other question, however, should never be obscured or forgotten by the answer concerning the hope of the individual. The other and more fundamental question concerns what we can say concretely about the hope for the future of mankind. Without it, the answer concerning the destiny of each individual within history does not completely make sense.

Jesus was able to preach about the coming Reign or Kingdom of God without explaining what he meant by the term because Israel had long been reflecting on the meaning of its own history as a people summoned by God to put itself under his rule or kingship. That reflection always centered on the experience of Exodus under the leadership of Moses.

Israel looked back—and does so now—and saw its origin as a people in a vocation to freedom from oppression by outsiders—a very earthy, politico-socio-economic understanding of redemption and salvation. That first liberation is portrayed not simply as the gift of God but as the demand of God upon his people, his command to them, a command to the impossible. Israel also looked back—and does so now—to the desert experience and the mysterious Sinai event of the covenant of God with his people—a liberation from the chaos of lawlessness and selfishness and oppression within the people itself when it opens itself to the sharing of God's creative and redemptive wisdom. There seem to be two recurring phases of liberation: 1- the throwing off of the false and oppressive rule that is alien since each man is in the image of God, and no man has his true end in the utility or convenience of another; and 2- the establishment in its place of the rule of God with all the changes of priorities and values that this requires.

Israel's accounts of the Sinai covenant give some ideas of the changes of priorities and values that are required. God will vindicate those who do not take advantage of the poor, the stranger, the widow, and the orphan but who act justly towards all. He will bless those who do not kill or destroy others nor covet what is theirs and those who honor their parents and the elders and those who teach their children the right way. He will show his wisdom and his mercy to those who worship him with a passion, tolerating no false gods, never invoking his name for what ultimately is untruth or trivial and making time and space in their lives to enter into dialogue with God as he progressively reveals himself.

To this covenant relationship the prophets of Israel tended to give a special slant that presented God as the Father and protector of the poor, of minorities and oppressed groups, and of all the weak or powerless. They also formulated some poetic projections of what it would be like when God truly and fully reigned among men. There would be a peace so profound that men would recycle the whole armory of slaughter-power into the tools of agricultural productive power (swords into plowshares, spears into pruning hooks). There would be a decent livelihood and dignity and independence for all (each man sitting in the shade of his own olive tree and by his own vineyard). There would be no more need for the weak to fear the strong (the wild animals from the mountains grazing in the fields with the flocks). All this would be because men would acknowledge but one God, the Lord of history and the guarantor of morality.

This picture may seem very sketchy, but it gives perfectly adequate guidance for a critique of any society. If there is war or armaments build-up, that must be changed. If there is poverty in the midst of wealth, that must be changed. If minorities and disadvantaged persons suffer, that must be changed. If men are alienated and oppressed by their work, reduced to a treadmill to make profit for others, that must be changed. If the powerless are oppressed or deprived with impunity, that must be changed. If men invoke the name of God for a little religiosity—done like a hobby one day a week—that is not allowed to challenge the values that reign over the real business of life with its social, economic, and political structures, that most assuredly must be changed. Otherwise, the Reign of God or Kingdom of Heaven comes no nearer.

This expectation offers—and always has—a very concrete hope. But it has its elusive side: When may it be expected to come about, and what is the action appropriate to that hope? We know that in the time of Jesus there already existed a teaching tradition of the inter-testamental period (between the last Hebrew Scriptures and the first New Testament writings). In those times of colonial domination, there was cause for extreme discouragement concerning the hope of Israel. There were those who felt that the two phases of the Exodus liberation would have to be reenacted in the same sequence. First, they would have to get the invaders out (by the time of Jesus, that meant the Romans). Israel then would be free to set its own house in order, establishing within its own people the Reign of God in the fullest sense. Others seem to have been ready to compromise, to give the kingship of God an extremely limited role in the world, accommodating themselves with no difficulty to situations of extreme injustice and oppression as though these were the norm. Still others seem to have concluded that the only solution was withdrawal into an isolated community that lived according to the revelation it had received. As always in such situations, there also were people who simply acknowledged the horror of the situation, assumed they could do absolutely nothing about it, and waited around for God to come in with a magic solution.

Yet there was a much more subtle teaching of the rabbis for those who had ears to hear it. On the one hand, they could but reassert the power of God over all the forces of the world—military, political, economic. God would come swiftly, suddenly, in his own way and in his own time, to vindicate those faithful to him, to manifest his power in the world, to establish his reign forever among men. On the other hand, their teaching to the individual was to live now under the kingship of God, to take upon himself the yoke of God's rule, and to acknowledge no other sovereign. In times of foreign domination, that might require heroism, even death rather than violate the law of God to obey the laws of princes. If a person takes upon himself the yoke of God's kingship, he enters into a dialogue of revelation in which he sees the reign of God coming. His living of the kingship of God in his own life is its own reward.

This view would seem to be an interpretation of the liberation theme of Exodus that puts the sequence the other way around. Rather than suggest that it is first necessary to chase out or to destroy the alien power by fighting those who wield that power, it seems to suggest that it is first necessary to put one's own house in order, to change one's values and priorities in response to God's revelation. In so doing, one very well may be brought into head-on confrontation with the foreign oppressor and may even have to choose death rather than infidelity to the revelation of God.

When we read the New Testament and reflect on the Christian community's understanding of what Jesus preached and why he died, it appears that neither the idea of the Reign of God nor the concrete content of that hope was original to Jesus. Careful reading of the gospel accounts of the preaching of Jesus suggests that they do not teach a new understanding of the action appropriate to that hope. The preceding paragraph seems to describe very well the stance that the gospels show us as that of Jesus. What does seem to be new in the teaching of Jesus is the timetable, the urgency of the call, and the immediacy of the promise. What seems to be new in the apostolic teaching is the focus on the person of Jesus as making all the difference. In the death of Jesus and the mysterious experience of the Resurrection, the Apostles found that power went out from him for the redemption of the world from all its woes. They tell us that this "mind-blowing" experience seemed to open their eyes, as though for the first time, to an understanding of all that Moses and the prophets had taught and to the personal realization of the nearness of the Reign of God and the fulfillment of creation and human history. It gave them an immediate and concrete understanding of the content of the hope. It also gave them the classic experience of the fidelity of God to the one who dies in his service, bringing about his reign among men.

The Church is simply those who were transformed by the

experience of the death and Resurrection of Jesus and who rallied to deepen their understanding of it in the celebration of Eucharist and in a community life that assumed the yoke of God's reign as they understood it, constituting themselves as his witness people, anticipating the end-goal of the Kingdom of God among all men. The Church frequently falls far short of this vision, but this is its true reality, what it is trying to be, what constitutes it as Church.

What we have to pass on in our tradition—the proper core of content for all Christian religious education—is this visionary hope. Clearly, description is not enough to pass it on. The hope came alive for the Apostles because of their experience of Jesus. Unlike the preaching of Jesus himself, which the gospels focus on the Reign of God, the preaching of the Apostles focuses on Jesus as the Christ. That basically is the good news they had to tell. When we ask how they passed on the experience, the New Testament itself tells us it was by the transformation in themselves, that the only proof of the Resurrection they could offer was the profound change in those who claimed to have experienced it. This certainly has always been true in some measure. The guarantee of the truth of the Christian claim—that is, of the trustworthiness of that visionary hope—is the transformed life of those who live by that hope and who already taste its fulfillment in anticipation.

It is clear, however, that since early in the history of the Church, this luminously self-validating quality could not be found in all Christians, perhaps not even in the majority. Very early, the teachers and preachers often had to rely not on their own transformed lives but on the explosive lives and deaths of heroes in the community. There was soon a cult of martyrs, of those who died a witness death, whose actions and words were treasured; their letters were read again and again in the churches in an effort to bring the people in touch with truly transfigured Christian lives. Later, there was the cult of confessors, who had suffered imprisonment and torture as testimony to the reality of their hope. To this witness we added those who remained virgins all their lives in testimony to the reality of their hope and those who embodied the concern and care of God for the poor, the orphaned, the imprisoned, the slaves, the minorities, and the oppressed of their society and time.

What we have to pass on, the central content of our tradition, is a great visionary hope brought alive in the experience of people transformed by it. It can be made meaningful only by contact with people transformed by it. We gain understanding and confidence and further guidance in the action appropriate to the great hope from the cumulative experience of the community that has tried, with greater or lesser fidelity, to live by it. But we cannot pass along uncritically everything that that community and its members and institutional structures have done. We are engaged necessarily in a constant process of discernment, meditating on Jesus Christ as presented to us in the gospels, and scrutinizing what goes on in the community in the light of Jesus Christ. Such a process of discernment is cumulative, and through it we gradually build a history of hope and heroes that is the proper heritage of new generations of Christians.

NOTES

A clear and detailed account of the Reign of God as the theme that provides continuity or coherence to the whole Bible is given in *The Kingdom of God* by John Bright (Abingdon Press, 1953).

Detailed documentation on the inter-testamental rabbinic teaching concerning the kingship of God is given in *Bible Key Words* edited by Gerhard Kittel, volume II (Harper & Row, 1958). This book, however, would be tedious reading with much guess-work for anyone who does not read Greek and a little Hebrew. It is mentioned here, nevertheless, because it gives such extraordinary insights into key words of the New Testament.

I have discussed how personal experience is expanded by empathy in my earlier book *The Meaning of the Sacraments* (Pflaum/Standard, 1972), chapter 3. For that reason, I have not repeated it here, though it is an essential link in the handing on of the experience as here described.

CHAPTER 4:
THE BOOKS OF THE PROMISE

Like all the great religions of the world, Christianity very early crystallized its message in certain written testimonies, though it was only gradually that the community came to an official canon listing what constituted its sacred Scriptures. In the long history of attempts to formulate in words the hope and experience of the Christian community, there are no words as central or important as the words that make up the collection of our sacred Scriptures, the Bible. Yet there is considerable ambivalence today among Catholic religious educators concerning the role of the Bible in the task of handing on the Catholic heritage.

If we are dealing with a long-standing tradition, it is certainly important for any proper understanding of it that we study carefully the testimonies that stand closest to the source and more particularly those that have been tried and tested and in retrospect have been acknowledged as central and trustworthy by those who have lived within the tradition. This is precisely what we have in the Bible. It is also important that those testimonies should not be handed over naked and without context, as though the books that make up the Bible could speak for themselves without further introduction, to all cultures and all ages. They must be offered in a context that gives meaning—that gives the meaning that these books have for the Church.

This task is delicately balanced, a task in which we seem rather frequently to have lost the balance, at least in modern times. On the one hand, we have had a rather dreadful experience of the Bible used as a treasure chest for proof texts. This has happened wherever an author approached the Scripture with the answer to his question already complete from other, later sources in the tradition, usually an authoritative (*magisterial*) statement of council, Pope, or synod; sometimes a formulation in a traditional creed or prayer formula. Such an author would pounce upon the Bible as though it were a rummage box, sorting his way through the scraps until he found one that more or less would fit his argument or would sanction his conclusion. In the process, these scraps of Scripture, taken out of context, were being made to express very different messages than those intended by the original authors, without anyone's being aware of it. This practice could only be called a prostitution of the Scriptures and scarcely could serve the purpose of building up the faith of the community and its visionary hope and its commitment to appropriate action. It scarcely could serve this purpose simply because the treasure chest, proof-text game is one that each player can play to his own advantage, as anyone who has had an argument with a fundamentalist well knows.

Such a situation, from which most of us have suffered, was intolerable. On the other hand, a swing to the other extreme, as has happened in recent years, has not been particularly helpful either. It seems that we now are suffering from a destructive sophistication complex. Having rediscovered the importance of ascertaining the meaning of the original author and the difficulty of that task, we may be in danger of a very profound discouragement concerning the spiritual or Christian relevance of the Scriptures today. It frequently appears that the Scripture scholarship that the Catholic community so urgently needs—and of which we were for some time so painfully deprived—now is reaching the community in sensational spurts, frequently out of context of the scholarly background, sometimes in bombastic and destructive utterances, and sometimes with a pseudo-sophistication that consists of slinging highly specialized vocabulary around.

We are in a predicament because most good Scripture scholars are reluctant to popularize their findings. The main reasons probably are three. First, the training of Scripture scholars does not incline them naturally towards broad, sweeping explanations but towards very painstaking, detailed work; this, in turn, tends to foster a special reluctance to venture beyond the field of their special competence in order to draw even some tentative conclusions for theologians, preachers, and Christian activists. Second, Scripture scholarship is so complex; so much has been done so fast in our times that many Scripture scholars seem extremely cautious about premature popularizations of their work lest they might introduce unnecessary confusion and anxiety for the community of believers. A third reason, more problematic than the other two, is that there still is a good deal of hierarchic vigilance exercised by persons who themselves were trained in the era of the treasure-chest, proof-text game, who personally have not yet tripped over the scandals of that way of treating Scripture and therefore cannot understand what is going on presently in genuine Scripture scholarship and are not able to distinguish it easily from destructive sensationalism. Unfortunately, while it lasts and wherever it is the case, this disposition can only reinforce the Scripture scholar's other two reasons for reluctance and therefore can only serve to widen the scope for more destructive and pseudosophisti-cated sensationalism.

This situation is one with which we may have to live for some time, and the question remains for those of us who are not Scripture specialists—but for whom the Scriptures are central to our work—as to how we can best hand on the Cath-olic heritage and work creatively within it. Certainly the best way is not to avoid the Scriptures, as is sometimes done, where Christianity is presented as though it might best be un-derstood from contemporary films or poetry, from existential-ist philosophy, or from classical Greek tragedy, or from spon-taneous reactions of a group of adolescents to their immediate experience. Nor is it helpful to proceed in teaching or preaching in the way that is legitimate for the Scripture scholar. To try to ascertain what we can find out about the meaning of the original author and then abruptly to stop is to fall short in most cases of the meaning that the Church has found. To concentrate on how little we can know of the origi-nal meaning and on how the Church's use of texts has differed from the original meaning is simply destructive of our sources for Christian life. More than this is wanted.

To know how to avail ourselves of the Bible in the handing on of the heritage, it is perhaps important to recall the func-tion of the Bible as Bible. The reasons for which individual books were written and the uses to which they were first put vary widely. But the purpose for which they are collected into a canon of sacred Scripture is fairly simple. They are gath-ered to be the text for community reading and meditation in public worship and are therefore the central resource for pri-vate meditation and for the building up of a common lan-guage of faith and of prayer. This was true for the Hebrew Scriptures long before the time of Jesus, probably about four centuries before Jesus as far as the central collection of the Pentateuch, or first five books, is concerned.

Israel established a pattern for prayer, for entering into dialogue with God who reveals himself, that is so natural that one might look at it and not notice it. In any literal sense, we cannot "see" or "hear" God. Our experience is always that of an absence rather than a presence, in the strict sense of that word. What we can see is the effect of God in our own lives, in the lives of others, and in the world. But this perception requires a certain sensitivity, a certain openness to God revealing himself, a worldview and a set of expectations that allow for the wonderful, the new. It is possible to look at almost any situation and see it in a purely secular way and to look at the same situation and see in it the hand of God. This would be true of the beauty of scenery, the unexpected resolution of a difficult human situation, an exceptionally good harvest, and so on.

There are people for whom nothing is wonderful, and therefore there is no cause for gratitude and the sense of receiving the good things of life without merit. In turn, then, there is no cause for compassion or generosity or graciousness to others. There is cause, rather, for dogged selfishness and exclusiveness with the good things of life because the only hope a man has for the future is what springs from his efforts on his own behalf. He sees community as an alliance of persons clustered into an interest group in order to assert themselves jointly against others. Loyalty to the group is a virtue because it "pays off." Consideration of those outside the group may be seen as a betrayal because "we have a duty to see to our own business."

There are, on the other hand, people who are very sensitive to the gift-like quality of so much that happens in their lives. They are aware that life itself—good health and intelligence and education and a good start on life and a childhood lived in peace and plenty—are all totally undeserved in the very nature of the case. They experience this and much else as gift, as providence of a gracious God and of other men who live in covenant with a gracious God. Their lives and actions seem to spring from gratitude and bear fruit in unselfish generosity.

For them, the gift naturally becomes the obligation. For them, the first order of business always is concern for those most in need, not a calculation of who is "deserving," or who is "on the right side" or "one of us."

For those who believe in a redeemer God acting in history, as Israel has believed as long as it has been a people, it becomes a highly significant question to find the means of cultivating the second outlook described above, not only in those who are predisposed by temperament and by fortunate experiences of love and friendship but in a whole people so that it may be handed on as that people's special heritage. It is important to discover by what means one comes to see the hand of God in one's life and in the life of the people, by what means one comes to experience the call of God in ordinary happenings in one's life and in the life of the people. It is essential to learn by what means one can develop sensitivity and proper discernment for the mysterious calls of God to new and undreamed-of possibilities.

In the worship and observances of Israel, one principle seems dominant. To see the hand of God in the present and to know where the finger of God beckons into the future, one must look back to where we know God has passed, to try to see him from behind since we cannot see his face. And we know where he has passed because his wonderful names resound through the world from those moments and events. Those names are mercy, where it was not deserved; compassion, where it could not have been expected (Exodus 33:18-23). The worship and observances of Israel, therefore, were built around the classic events that radically changed Israel's capacity for perception of its world and its history and its future, the great revelatory happenings in which, in retrospect, the hand of God could be discerned so clearly.

The basic pattern of worship and observances became the commemoration of such an event in dramatic action (ritual), story, and song of praise and thanksgiving. That is the pattern of the Passover Seder, of the Feast of Tabernacles, and so on. That is also, though more diffusely, the pattern of the Sabbath. For Christians, this pattern was adopted in the Eucharist, or reenactment of the Lord's Supper, and in the great feasts of Easter, Pentecost, Epiphany, Christmas. The purpose of such a commemoration was not only to remember in the common sense of that word but to "recall"—to make the event present again by the community's present participation in it. This often meant, and does today mean, the effort to make the event present in ways and depths in which it has not been present before, to try to penetrate deeper into the understanding of it on the basis of all the community's efforts to date to live out the implications of its previous understanding.

For this purpose, "story" clearly does not mean an accurate recall of the factual data observed at the time nor the concern at least to get an eyewitness account of the event. "Story" here is necessarily interpretive. It assumes a backward look to an event that may not even have been appreciated as the work of God at the time but from which the power and graciousness of God radiate out in retrospect. It requires a contemplation of the event in this light, a meditation upon it in terms of its implications for the present and for God's call to this community into the future. In other words, "story" normally will not be a simple recital of the facts but a complex, interpretive account stressing the aspects that are significant for the community in the present, the aspects that throw light on the universal human situation and on God's liberating power within that situation. In one sense, the Bible as a collection of texts for reading and meditation at liturgies is full of stories and utterances that stand in their own right without reference to any specific history, stories rich in symbolism and open-ended in their meaning and implications. It is very important to read such stories not for information but for insight. In another sense, however, it was and is crucial to Israel's understanding and use of its Scriptures that they do present a very specific history of the redeeming intervention of God in the history of this particular people, binding them to particular observances in pursuit of what had been revealed to them at very clearly specified moments in their history. It is this particularity that always has presented and does now present the great scandal of Israel, the People, the Land, and the Law.

The Christian canon of Scripture, like the Hebrew canon, has grown out of the selection of writings for use in public worship. The early Christian communities built their worship around the Hebrew Scriptures, reinterpreting them in the light of their explosive revelatory experience of the Resurrection of Christ. Only gradually did the community write, collect, and select its own Christian Scriptures, written and chosen by people steeped in the heritage of the Hebrew Scriptures and the Hebrew tradition and making solid sense only to readers and listeners who likewise can fill in this background. This point seems to be rather crucial for the handing on of the characteristic heritage of Christians. It does not explain itself but always becomes abstract, elusive, and artificial if not experienced and explained in the context of the Hebrew tradition and expectation and of the Hebrew Scriptures with their wealth of stories, prototypes, wisdom, poetry. Generally today among Catholic religious educators, the embarrassment felt about the place of the Bible in general is more acute concerning the place of the Hebrew Scriptures (or Old Testament) in the task of religious education; there is a tendency to present the gospels as though they spoke for themselves without reference to the Hebrew Scriptures.

The Bible, for Christians as for Jews, is, on the one hand, free of history, full of stories and utterances that speak in their own right; but, on the other hand, it is dependent upon and concerned with a very specific history. The scandal of Christianity always has been and now is the particularity of the claims it makes about Jesus as the Christ, his role as redeemer of the world, and his unique relationship to the transcendent God, Father of all men. The meaning of Christianity simply cannot be understood by down-playing this particularity, hoping everything somehow will fall into place by itself. The Bible is at the core of our tradition; that is, it crystallized out of the early expressions of the community's experience within that tradition and then became a very active force within that tradition, shaping it and challenging the shape of it. Whenever the tradition is to be handed on, that is to say, wherever tradition is to happen in Christian circles, the Bible must be at the center of it, but the Bible in the sense in which it was collected and placed in the center in the first place.

The Bible in religious education has to be offered as an invitation to enter into the dialogue with God revealing himself in the midst of the People of God, the community with its whole experience, its whole history of response and non-response, and with its scandalous particularity. The theme of the Bible is the particularity and discernibility of God's intervention in the history of men and the universal implications of this series of particular interventions.

Because the Bible is this type of collection of texts, its meaning is always more than the intent of the original author of a particular passage. The true meaning of a text includes everything that caused it to be included in the canon of Scripture. It also includes all the shades and nuances and connotations that the text takes on in the context of all the rest of Scripture. The Christian meaning of a text also includes the effect it has had on the shaping of the community and its history and tradition. Anyone who has read extensively in the Christian literature of the patristic age cannot but be aware that the Bible for the churches of that time was not a dead word, spoken long ago, but a living word spoken by the living God in the present in the living community.

The question for our time is how that sense of immediate presence and creative, active participation in the word of God in Scripture can be recovered. Certainly it cannot be done by naiveté about the changing meaning of words and recitals or by unconcern for the original meaning of the author of each passage. Nor can it be done by sheer scholarly retrieval efforts. It can really only be done by being steeped in the symbols and stories of the tradition so that the language of the Bible becomes the language of wrestling with present problems. This task requires extensive exposure to and reflection on the whole Bible and on much extra-biblical legend and folklore that develops biblical themes or incidents. Then the Bible and its symbolism and its view of history become an integrated interpretation of reality into which any new experience or question may be introduced and within which it comes into focus and acquires clearer meaning. This is a goal toward which religious education must strive, because this is the point at which a Christian's life becomes open to God revealing himself within the context of the people, where the revelation can be received and shared and acted upon.

The matter remains difficult for most religious educators. Because, for the most part in our generation, we have not been steeped in the stories and symbols of our Scriptures as matured in the living tradition, there is a great sense of awkwardness and distaste for the presentation of Scripture in the processes of religious education, formal and informal, in classroom and in preaching, both with children and with adults. Everyone thinks it would probably be good to "bring in an expert sometime to get the scriptural base straight." But the tendency is for those who are responsible for the task of handing on the heritage to feel incompetent themselves and for those who are called in to be too specialized and unprepared to make a presentation of Scripture as read and meditated and lived by the community up to today. This, however, is in any case only part of the problem; such a presentation can be made only in the context of a community that presently, constantly meditates and consciously lives the Scriptures.

When such a community experience is not available for participation, the telling of the "story" will always seem remote from real life and from significant issues. The Christian community cannot be shaped without the Scriptures. If present interest and sense of immediacy and relevance are missing, the bridge must be built to the point at which they can be retrieved. Some groping and bridge-building probably has to take place at all levels. Certainly all those who are responsible for handing on the tradition must be engaged in a personal discovery of the language and worldview of the Bible within the Church, primarily by constantly meditating and reading the whole Bible, and, secondly, by studying the results of biblical scholarship easily available today. In this way, the selections read and meditated in the liturgy acquire a three-dimensional character quite different from the flat and unreal impression they give when simply taken out of context. From this vantage point, it should be possible to invite the Christian community at large—not only the handful who eagerly frequent adult education programs—to a more extensive reading and meditation of Scripture. Given that our Sunday Eucharist is so short when compared, for instance, with a Jewish Sabbath morning service and the readings covered in such a service, it would seem appropriate for those who preach every Sunday to more or less the same congregation to propose preparatory reading for the following week's discussion. No doubt such good suggestion would fall in some places on stony ground, or on shallow soil or where it is easily snatched away again; but any that fell on good ground surely would yield a hundredfold for the Church community as a whole.

There appears today to be great readiness and eagerness for lay study groups, such as Bible study and meditation and prayer groups. There also appears to be considerable anxiety about the possible errors or dangers of such groups. There certainly are reasons to fear the use of creative imagination within the Christian community today, especially in regard to the interpretation of the Scriptures. We have not yet disentangled from the Catholic-Protestant controversy about private interpretation. We also have been so far adrift from our biblical and liturgical roots that reflections on Scripture offered by individual laymen in such groups frequently are shallow, moralistic, and sometimes demonstrably incorrect. Yet there is no way to learn to meditate Scripture other than to start doing it with what help is available and to reflect on each passage in the light of what is known of the whole and as a critique of the praxis of this community here and now as it tries to live out its commitment to Christ.

An important element to recapture seems to be the art of storytelling, of reading aloud so as to allow mysteries to be revealed, and of retelling the story so that it becomes the story of the present. In this the Catholic tradition is very rich, but the present Catholic community is impoverished. For some centuries, we had a certain mistrust of the words of Scripture read in their own right and privately meditated. At the same time, we developed a formal and official theology that not only was remote from the Bible but remote from the real life and language of real people and real problems. That left the traditions of spirituality to find support and sustenance without much help from Scripture or theology, and we had petty spirituality traditions sometimes using a shallow and sentimental symbolism, splintering into groups that barely spoke one another's symbol language.

We now have many legends of the saints, presenting the wonderful works of God in the context of different cultures and societies; but we are embarrassed and hampered somewhat by the emotional particularity of the style and language. It will take much effort to discover and to draw to the forefront the legends and stories that have classic simplicity and can speak universally. At present, we do not have good roots in the creative imaginings of our own more recent tradition, and therefore we have difficulty in finding access to the story-telling styles and idioms of the Bible. Find it we must. Without it we lose the substance of what it is we have to hand on to succeeding generations.

Probably the most helpful way to recover freedom and familiarity with our own symbols and stories is to look at the way other traditions use theirs. Hinduism, for instance, not only has handed on a great heritage through myriad streams and channels, but it has had so much written about it in the West that it has become easily accessible. Much closer to home are various strands within Judaism, particularly the colorful patterns of life, thought, and expression of the Hassidim of Eastern Europe, whose doings and sayings have become subject matter for many collections and anthologies that make them also very accessible to the interested outsider. From reading accounts of the symbolism of another tradition, one often may gain fresh and deep insights into the language of one's own faith tradition.

NOTES

For a consideration of the function of the Bible and its meaning to the Christian community, *Introducing the Bible* by William Barclay (Abingdon Press, 1972), though written by a Protestant for Protestant readers, should prove extremely helpful to Catholics.

Most of the material of this chapter rests on key ideas in the documents of Vatican II, more particularly *Sacrosanctum Concilium, The Constitution on the Sacred Liturgy.*

The stories and doings of the Hassidim have been recorded by Martin Buber, Abraham Heschel, and others, and they are easily available in Schocken paperbacks. Very readable is

Elie Wiesel's *Souls on Fire* (Random House, 1972).

Probably the most helpful book on the New Testament is *This Man Jesus,* by Bruce Vawter (Doubleday).

CHAPTER 5:
FOLKLORE AND FANTASY

Many of us in the present generation of Catholics are quite embarrassed and ill at ease with the folklore and fantasy of our tradition. Miracle stories, whimsical saints, visions and locutions, stories of sudden healing and conversion have difficulty in finding a place in our recollection of the history of our people. This attitude seems to be related to our understanding of truth. In general, in our society and culture, we equate truth with the empirically verifiable. One ought to be able to experiment and produce the same results, or one should be able to check it out with disinterested and therefore reliable witnesses.

Religious faith necessarily uses a language of suggestion rather than of unambiguous, descriptive statement. Faith statements are never empirically verifiable. One cannot experiment in the ordinary sense of the word. Moreover, there simply are no disinterested witnesses; those who stand outside the experience of which the statement is made are not witnesses at all. They cannot testify; they have not seen or heard anything. Those who stand inside an experience for which a religious claim is made experience it in terms of their own acceptance or rejection of the claim that is made on them personally. Whether they accept or reject, they are not disinterested witnesses.

If our understanding of truth is limited to the empirically verifiable, then the language of religious faith makes claims that are neither true nor untrue. We cannot place God under a microscope or at the end of a telescope. We cannot run experiments to reproduce grace or love or repentance or forgiveness. What we can do is to hint at the realities of which we speak, which are always greater than any words, which lie at the very boundary of what language can express. The language of such hinting is the language of poetry and of strong, classic drama. It is the language of the creative imagination when it is no longer cautiously walking along, testing the ground before putting a foot down. It is the language of the creative imagination when it dances and eventually just flies.

In our traditions of spirituality, we have a great deal of such language, describing events in the relation of man to God in prayer and events in the relation of man to man in charity and compassion and loyalty. Stories of desert fathers directing their disciples to water dry sticks or great spiritual guides telling novices to plant things upside-down are, of course, simply silly to the literal mind, as are Joshua's trumpets around Jericho and the staff with which Moses struck the rock. To anyone with any sense at all of poetry and symbol, these are pregnant statements concerning a life that is lived by faith. A saint who refers to herself as a Little Flower and teaches a Little Way is nothing but an embarrassment within a mentality in which a flower is by definition trivial and peripheral and "little" means "not to be taken seriously."

One might add many more examples. A saint who refers to

animals and inanimate things as "brother" and "sister" would seem to be incapable of communicating with technological man, and one for whom constant miracles are claimed becomes simply incredible. Yet, if we can break through the cultural barriers of the different emotional tonality in which much of our spiritual traditions and our hagiography (our saint lore) is available, it often becomes so contemporary as to be frightening. The desert fathers have already passed 1984 and 2001. Thérèse Martin is far ahead of the drug scene. Francis of Assisi is after the ecological revolution. Women's liberation seems quaintly old-fashioned and unsure of itself beside persons like Bridget of Sweden and Catherine of Siena. We surely do not need to be ashamed of our saints, and in order to pass on the Catholic heritage, we must just as surely learn the idiom and style of hagiography.

Because Christianity is first and foremost life lived according to a visionary hope, the fundamental level of what has to be passed on of the experience of the ages is the story of the community's heroes, its saints. There is a reason for this. A saint is not someone who is judged or guaranteed to have sinned less than others nor even one who is judged to have lived by greater love. A saint basically is one in whom the meaning of Christ for a particular situation or society or time or problem has become startlingly, luminously visible. No matter how unconventional, controversial, and incomprehensible his life may have been to many while he was living it, in retrospect it is self-validating when seen by the light of Christ. Our process of canonization or saint-making is a cautious one that ensures this. Unfortunately, it is also sometimes so slow that by the time a saint is officially acclaimed, his contribution to Christian life and understanding has sometimes been so thoroughly assimilated or so much toned down and diluted that it is no longer evident how unconventional and controversial he was.

A spontaneous "cult" or hero worship usually springs up

first around a person recently dead or even around one still alive. The people who participate in such a cult are saying, in effect, that God has revealed himself to them anew in the life of this person so that their capacity for perception is transformed. They see what is going on in the world and hear the promise of God for the world differently because their lives have been touched by this person. Church authority, at different levels of the hierarchic structure, eventually becomes involved and must decide whether to impede, tolerate, or encourage such a cult. This represents a corporate effort at discernment and critique of Christian praxis. The key question is whether the meaning of Christ for the world is interpreted authentically by this life in such a way that we gain new understanding. This question is difficult to answer; there is no blueprint or slide rule by which to check it. "New understanding" means just that. The only criterion is whether the new insight or understanding gained is in harmony with the gospel of Christ as we have had it from the beginning and as we understand it through our own praxis. It assumes that those who must make the discernment have a deep, personal understanding, gained from the praxis of their own lives and that of the whole community, of the meaning of Christ for the world. It may be for this reason that the process sometimes is so slow that the originality and creativity of the life that is being examined begin to fade from view. It may be for this reason that in modern times the requirement of attested miracles has become central to the process of canonization.

To many of us today, the whole question of miracles has become a nagging problem. That may be because we think of a miracle primarily as an event that cannot be explained in natural terms, that is, as an event that contradicts the laws of nature as we know them from the natural sciences. The definition is self-defeating. It begs the question of whether anything ever may be said to contradict the laws of nature, or of whether we always should take note that we have not yet correctly assessed the laws of nature when they present us with a "surd." If we try to check out miracles of healing according to the definition just given, it becomes impossible; the effort always raises the question whether there is a closer, more direct or more complex relationship between mind and body than we have yet been able to grasp conceptually.

Miracles might better be defined as those truly outstanding, wonderful works of God in which his power and his mercy are revealed anew so that people are able to transcend themselves, to make a leap beyond their petty present situation because they see the coming of the new heaven and the new earth, and therefore they see the possibilities for the future of mankind greatly expanded from the little we usually dare to hope and to do. In this sense, of course, miracles must be required as conditions for canonization. Unless such wonderful works of God have appeared from the life of an individual, he really cannot be held up to the community as revealing in a new way the meaning of Christ for the world.

Yet a miracle in this sense may be difficult to describe, and surely it cannot be empirically verified. The attitude and response of the community of believers are constitutive factors in this definition of miracle. As the New Testament reminds us, even if one should rise from the dead, the response of the unbeliever is simply to comment that the death certificate seems to have been a mistake. One has to be open to the breaking of the power of God into one's life and world before the wonderful works of God can come about. Jesus himself is reported as being unable to do such wonderful works for some groups of people because of their hardness of heart, which excluded all possibility of a wonderful breakthrough.

Miracles are not magic. Neither for Jesus nor for the saints of Christian tradition has it been claimed that they did magic. Magic has nothing to do with religious faith. It is sub-personal, manipulative. It assumes the very opposite of a personal God who is the Father of men and the Lord of all history. It assumes that ultimate reality consists of contradictory, irrational, and impersonal forces that can be manipulated by learning tricks. Because Catholic tradition is so full of miracle stories, it is important that we neither devalue them nor confuse them with magic. Miracles are personal. They are the wonderful works of God whose power and mercy break open new possibilities in apparently hopeless situations because of a conversion of men's hearts. Miracles happen among believers, and they are of many kinds, as many kinds as there are humanly hopeless situations in which men are oppressed and diminished in their humanity and their power to respond to God as their ultimate liberating goal.

In a community of believers, of course, miracles should be happening constantly. Yet it is difficult to cultivate that openness to the call of God and to the demands of our faith that makes it possible for the wonderful works of God to be done among us. It means maintaining a worldview, or frame of reference, that expects such interventions and new possibilities, and it means living out the implications of that worldview. This is why the folklore of saints and of wonderful happenings is so important to the handing on of the Christian heritage. And this is why the whole heritage of Christian experience through the ages must be drawn into our celebration.

Our basic pattern of worship, like that of Israel, is a celebration; we recall a past event, making it present again by our participation in it. We contemplate such an event and meditate on the meaning of it, seeing it clearly in retrospect as a wonderful act of God. From looking at it in the past, we learn to discern the wonderful acts of God in our present world and to know what is the invitation of God into the future. For us, the classic event is the Paschal Mystery of the death and Resurrection of Christ, which we celebrate explicitly in the Eucharist, to which all the other sacraments and celebrations are closely linked.

We attempt to penetrate deeper into the mystery of Jesus Christ in his saving death and Resurrection by meditating on the Scriptures as we come to celebrate the Eucharist. In the gospel readings, we spell out not only the events of the Paschal Mystery itself but stories and sayings designed to explain what it was that Jesus taught, the impact he had on people, and just whom we understand him to be. In the other Scripture readings, we supply the whole historical, symbolic, ritual, and doctrinal background in which the life and death of Jesus were set and within which they must be viewed and understood. But we do not stop with the Scriptures of the New Testament. By linking the Eucharistic celebration with the anniversaries of martyrs' deaths (from very early times), and with the festivals of saints (from somewhat later times), our tradition has suggested that the meaning of the life and death of Jesus for the world must also be read and understood in the light of the difference it has made in history since that time. Through canonized saints and their commemoration, there is a process of interpretation going on throughout the Christian centuries of the meaning of the gospel in different social contexts and circumstances. When we link this process with our Eucharistic celebration, we are also recalling these lives, seeing in them in retrospect the wonderful works of God in order to be able more clearly to discern the call of God in the present. We examine them to acquire a sensitivity to the ways in which the power and mercy of God break through in history.

Clearly, the very brief references to the saints that are made in the Eucharistic liturgies on their feast days barely would be able to carry such enlightenment. The folklore and fantasy that Christian recollection has built around these persons are immensely important and have to be passed on elsewhere, the more so as most Catholics do not participate in weekday liturgies, and commemorations of the saints seldom occur on Sundays. Religious education is the process of tradition formalized and made self-conscious; it is not adequate if it does not put coming generations and newcomers in the adult community in touch with this great wealth of illuminating examples of what the gospel of Jesus Christ can mean in terms of creative living in a world that has not yet accepted the Reign of God.

As in the case of the Bible, the question of meaning and how it is determined is crucial here. The purpose of recalling the lives of the saints is not to retrieve the factual information as completely and accurately as possible. Such information retrieval is important, but it is only a small contribution to the task. The recollections and tellings of such lives by the community always have been interpretive, and sometimes this interpretive style has been lavish in its use of hyperbole and metaphor. It is not enough to try to strip it away to "get at the facts" because an important aspect of the message is contained in that lavish style. It is necessary to relearn the language of poetry and fairy tale and myth, because we are at the boundary of language in the subject matter that we are trying to discuss.

Because Christianity is above all the pursuit of a visionary hope rather than a set of beliefs, there is no better or more fundamental way to learn or to explain what it is about than in a series of living examples, stretching from Christian origins to our own present world context. From this exercise, principles of Christian spirituality can be derived, and against this background, creedal statements of Christian faith and systematic elaborations of such statements can begin to make sense.

NOTES

Helpful literature on the saints and the tradition of spirituality written for the contemporary reader is admittedly rare. Extraordinary insights often are gained by tracing the influence of the lives of the saints in the lives of outstanding and exceptionally creative, courageous Christians of our time.

Some of the ideas presented here are developed or at least adumbrated in a great variety of essays by Karl Rahner concerning Ignatius of Loyola, the Spiritual Exercises of Ignatius, devotion to the Sacred Heart, and the cult of saints in general, e.g. in *Theological Investigations,* Volume III (Helicon, 1967), in *The Dynamic Element in the Church* (Herder, 1964), and in *The Christian in the Market Place* (Sheed & Ward, 1966).

The basic theory of this chapter is the theology of revelation in the focus that has become general since Vatican Council II. I have not developed it here because it is discussed in chapter II of my book *What Are the Theologians Saying?* (Pflaum, 1970).

CHAPTER 6:
CRITIQUE OF PRAXIS

The process of canonization of saints, as described in the last chapter, is an example of the Catholic community engaging in a critique of praxis. It is not the only example, but it is a helpful one. The canonization process acknowledges that not everything that exists in the Church ought to be and that what ought to be is rare and must be discovered carefully.

Neither the code nor the creed nor the cult of Christians was spelled out from the beginning. The beginning was the experience of a great promise and the response of a great hope, leading to a process of creative attempts to live by that hope and that promise. Such creative efforts must be evaluated by those who attempt them by examining the outcomes in the light of the goal and in terms of their inner coherence. Under such scrutiny, some creative attempts were repudiated from early times—for example, the voluntary seeking out of martyrdom for the faith and the imposition of celibacy on all Christians. Other attempts were endorsed, such as missionary journeys to communities that had issued no invitation and voluntary dedication of one's lifelong virginity to the urgent quest of the Reign of God in the world.

Every time such decisions are made, the community is compelled to ask and to give reasons for these decisions. Those reasons, to be satisfactory to the community, have to invoke what is already the agreed understanding of the community's hope and beliefs and commitment to action. Every time such reasons have to be given, it is because the community of believers has been confronted with a new question to which it has no formulated answer as yet. Every time such reasons have to be given, there is some sort of struggle within the community of believers to go back over its history to find the common ground for a decision. Therefore, in every such case, there results some sort of rehearsal of what the community hopes and believes.

In the long run, there are two ways that such recitals of faith and hope are formulated. On the one hand, there is a strong drive to logical coherence of the worldview, the understanding of man and of all reality, that is expressed, because one cannot satisfactorily live and decide by a vision that is not coherent. On the other hand, there is an equally strong drive towards practical relevance. No matter how coherent an understanding of reality may be, if it does not "work" in practice it is useless.

There are various ways in which a faith formulation might not "work." If, for instance, it claims to answer questions that are answered differently by science, the believer is in trouble. If it is concerned mainly with answering questions that no one is asking, it will be placed in a Sunday compartment of the believer's mind and will hardly be operative in his real decisions. If it is so formulated as to preclude important questions of value and purpose that people are currently asking, those who formerly were believers are likely to abandon the tradition and the community in despair. It is probably true to say that each of these problems is being experienced by considerable numbers of Catholics today.

Problems of this type seem to be experienced by contemporary Catholics for two reasons. On the one hand, there certainly has been in the life of the Church since the later Middle Ages a tendency to clericalize theology and therefore a tendency to emphasize the inner logical coherence at the expense of eliminating some crucial new questions as they have arisen from practical affairs and from new knowledge in natural science and other fields. The result is that what we have to hand on as the formulation of the Christian community's worldview is in many respects not up-to-date. It would be useless to expect at any time to hand on a finished product, rather than to wrestle anew with contemporary questions that seem to challenge everything from the foundations. It is not unrealistic, however, to suppose that one ought to be able to enter into the ongoing process that has been wrestling with the new questions arising up to the present. This is a modest and realistic expectation that cannot be fulfilled at present.

The second reason for the problem seems to lie in the way we have learned what was there to be handed on. On the whole, we have been introduced to creedal formulations as though they constituted a beginning and were intelligible in isolation from their history and context. The classic creedal formulations have, for the most part, not appeared as a critique of praxis, hammered out painfully as the outcome of the struggle to live the implications of the gospel. We have met them, rather, as though they were "first principles" that have always stood aloof, intact, beyond question, and from which all norms for Christian living and hoping and striving could be derived logically. Yet neither the way we have learned it nor the bias in modern theology towards logical coherence at the expense of practical relevance is true to the early development of the Christian tradition and its classic formulations.

Creedal formulations, especially the great classic ones, have arisen historically as a critique of praxis, and they will make sense if they are introduced as such. The same is true for all formulations of code and of the ritual for worship. The ancient catechumenate programs give us some practical examples. An initial stage was, and should be today, a quick sketch of what it is that Christians hope and why and an indication of how one lives by that hope. Only when a person has tried for some time to live so, and then returns asking for further instruction, is a formal catechumenate begun. Such a catechumenate proceeds by way of extensive assimilation of stories, symbols, prayers, reflections in Bible readings, and the telling of Christian history. It also includes gradual initiation into the community's worship celebrations with all their rich symbolism, and it includes further teaching concerning a morality for Christians. All this is included in what is summed up at the end in the baptismal creed.

Creeds were formulated in the early ages of the Christian community, sometimes by local communities and sometimes by councils of the universal Church, as a summary of the common basis on which the community's understanding rests. The earliest creeds stayed with the language and symbols of the Bible, offered little philosophical elaboration, and provided a general framework for a Christian view of man in relation to God, world, and history. The Apostles' Creed, as we now have it, may serve as an example, being very close to the ancient Roman creed.

That general framework is a crucial aspect of the Catholic heritage. In fact, it is like a hinge holding it together. It gives a perspective on God as mystery in the life of man. It in no way attempts a discussion of the inner reality of God, much less a definition of God. God is identified for us in the creeds in terms of history. First, there is the clarification that we are speaking of the transcendent God, the one and only God, Father of men, Lord of history, whom Israel has always worshipped and whom we know as taught to us by Israel. The creeds do not begin with a philosophical notion of God but with God as identified by events in history, the God of believers, God experienced as intervening in history.

The particular way that God is described in the first section of the creeds is already of the greatest significance in indicating the nature of the heritage that we are passing on. The description arose out of Israel's attempt to respond step-by-step to a mysterious call heard again and again by sensitive listeners among the people. The description shaped up the way it did strictly as a critique of praxis, always reflecting on experience and expressing what was learned from it in attempts to formulate the ideal relation of man to God and therefore the best ways of thinking about God. Moreover, this description was taken over by Christians as part of their official statement of faith because, in trying to live by the vision they had found in Jesus, they kept rediscovering the ancient formulation as expressing their own quest for God.

At the same time, the frame of reference offered us in the ancient creeds presents the mystery of God in a three-sided paradox. God has shown himself concretely, tangibly in human history, in the midst of human affairs, in the person of Jesus. Though we insist on the unity of God and the ultimate gracious harmony of all that is, we maintain doggedly that God is known both as transcendent, calling all history to its goal in the future, and as a tangibly present personal point in history defined by particulars. Likewise, we still maintain that the reality of God is known immediately in the Spirit of Jesus who is the Spirit of the followers of Jesus, forming the community in our own day and within our own experience.

Philosophically, logically, the frame of reference for reality and the perspective on God provided by the creeds will not hold together. It is not the logical coherence that has guided the formulation of this framework. It is, rather, fidelity to experience and to what has been learned from experience. The coherence that is there is the coherence of the words of faith with the history of the Christian community. This is to be said not only of the account of God as triune but also of the accounts of Jesus as triumphant in defeat, as exalted in his death, as Messiah though officially rejected by the authorities in Israel, and, most importantly, as genuinely and totally a man yet divine. There is no logical coherence in this presentation either. There is only the dogged fidelity to the truth apprehended by our experience as a community of believers. More particularly, there is the concern for formulations of Christology that undergird what we have recognized in the praxis of the community as the proper Christian hope and the action appropriate to that hope.

The same may be said again of the assertions made concerning the Spirit and the Church, concerning the hope and mystery of the world to come, and concerning the struggle in history that is to move us towards that future. This very brief and by no means self-explanatory section was hammered out centuries after the Christological section that is the core of any statement of Christian faith and after the adoption of the first section that simply was taken over from Israel. It was and is a cryptic summary of the agreed basis of our endeavor as Church, the terms of our cooperation as followers of Jesus. It is cryptic because it can have meaning only to those who have experienced the life of the Christian community and have engaged in a struggle to determine what are the hinges on which the life of the community turns, what in fact is holding everything together in the common effort that constitutes the community of Christians.

Because religious education is the process of tradition become self-conscious, the slogan-summaries that constitute our creeds must be an integral part of what is "handed over" in the religious education offered within the Catholic community. What is difficult is to do it with the subtlety and mastery of our tradition that this process requires. The creeds may not be laid out as a starting point from which explanations can be elaborated and all understanding can be reached. They must always be discovered anew in the process of religious education, at the end of the struggle to understand, as summarizing the contribution to understanding that we can draw from the experience and wisdom of the classic (patristic) age of our community's history. When they are rediscovered in this way, the meaning of the formulas is enlarged and acquires new implications and connotations. It is more than the meaning intended by the original authors.

This process, however, requires that religious educators and preachers be steeped in the tradition and have made such rediscoveries themselves constantly in order to guide others and to allow them some spontaneity in the questioning and the discovery of answers. This surely is the most difficult problem that has to be resolved concerning the content of religious education in the Catholic community today. It will never be resolved by textbooks; a textbook necessarily programs learning beforehand without reference to the particular learner or the particular situation. A catechist must be far more than a catechism and any teacher or preacher something quite other than text or textbook. What we need is a cadre of people who have personally participated in the building of the tradition so that they know its inner coherence in terms of life and life-decisions, people who can lead the newcomer and the questioner into the experiences and reflections of the community through the ages, in such a way that the questioner is pursuing his own real-life questions and discovering what the accumulated wisdom of the Christian community can contribute to the answering of his own real-life questions.

The training and preparation of such guides is a serious problem; it involves so much more than academic study. It involves a total commitment of personal resources to living out the implications of the gospel within the community with all its faults and limitations. This is the praxis out of which one can begin to participate in the shaping of the wisdom of the tradition. This has become additionally difficult in our times because of a modern gap in the active participation in shaping the tradition. For too long we have assumed that our role in tradition was simply to learn the ready-made formula and to pass it along as something static, timeless, self-contained, to be applied to life. Most preachers and teachers and catechists today assume that the tradition is shaped without them and that they are powerless, like a cork bobbing along on the stream. Many Catholics have assumed that the only active participant in the shaping of tradition in our days is the Pope. Yet modern popes frequently have written as though they saw themselves as equally passive, simply drawing the necessary logical conclusions from what previous popes or councils have said and written. There is a pervasive sense that it is all out of our hands and that we have no significant role to play.

Under such circumstances, there is bound to be a great unwillingness to resolve new questions and contemporary problems within the Church, that is, from the resources provided by the ongoing praxis of the community of believers as it now is and as it is linked with the past. Under such circumstances, there is a tendency to disinvolvement from the struggle, disinterest in the life and history and concerns of the Church community, and an inclination to try to "go it alone" with attempts at creating an instant love ethic, a new authenticity cult, self-directed trips into inner space. Preachers and teachers are very vulnerable to contemporary fads because they have lost confidence in the wealth of experience and wisdom built up over the ages by the community that has tried to live its life as one in Christ. There is a pervasive sense that one can probably understand and live the meaning of Jesus Christ much more authentically by skipping over the entire intervening history.

70

Yet creativity does not come from ignoring the past but from grasping it from within so as to catch visionary moments that reveal what can be done with the future. Creativity does not come from unschooled, primitive spontaneity but from highly disciplined mastery of the situation that allows for the acquisition of a sophisticated spontaneity. Our religious heritage in the Catholic community provides this, but we seem to have lost confidence that we can still reach it, and we are content therefore to let the heritage die and be embalmed.

The question for most Catholic catechists and preachers and teachers is how to recapture what they have never known nor seen in the Church as they have experienced it. The way back is bound to be quite long and arduous. Because the living reality is not readily accessible to most of us, we must get much of it from books. We need to saturate ourselves with the writings of the patristic era, particularly the Apostolic Fathers and second- and third-century writers because of the freshness and simplicity with which they engaged in the task of shaping the tradition in their day. We need to enter deeply into the history of doctrines and of spiritual traditions. Church history should not mean the history of hierarchic structures and their relations with the secular governments of their day. It must be a way of reliving the vital questions of Christian attempts to live by the vision we have in Jesus Christ.

In the ordinary process of religious education within the Catholic community, we can and must proceed by responding to the real-life questions of those who come to learn rather than by superimposing a ready-made scheme. But we can afford this necessary luxury only if we have a trained cadre of guides with an extensive historical and systematic foundation, persons who have made a long and disciplined study of the whole tradition without prejudging what is relevant. We need persons who will answer spontaneously from their personal experience and conviction with a breadth and sophistication that comes from a long and deep engagement with the experience and wisdom of the community through the ages. We have many programs for the formation of religious educators today, but for the most part they do not give us the kind of people described here. To learn the resources of the Catholic tradition takes a great deal of time and more than an academic investment.

In such an historic and systematic study, the shaping of the classic creeds is important, but to be able to share with others a vital and dynamic grasp of the creeds as the outcome of reflection on praxis, the religious educator himself must have a good grasp not only of the history of the shaping of the creeds but of the history of theology and of Christian thought in general. It is difficult, if not impossible, to understand and to evaluate any particular theological opinion or position if one is not acquainted with the process of theologizing from within in the context of the Church community and in considerable historical depth. Without this, criteria for discrimination are hard to come by; they tend to degenerate into an absolute value placed on contemporary hierarchic authority, or to reduce everything to logical coherence within one's own philosophical framework, or simply to be limited to what happens to be acceptable to one's target audience. None of these is an adequate criterion in catechesis or preaching because all three norms reduce theology to something less than the critique of the Christian community's praxis.

What has been said of creed and of the theological elaboration of creed also ought to be said of Christian morality and of the ritual structure. (The latter belongs in the following chapter.) Concerning Christian morality, many religious educators give the impression today that they do not believe that we have any Catholic treasury of wisdom to hand on. There are reasons for this impression, but it is nevertheless unfortunate and untrue. The reasons may have much to do with a general crisis of moral values and assumptions today that accompanies extremely rapid technological development and culture change and that is much wider than the Catholic community. They may also have much to do with the over-rigid attempts at codifying and classifying all human action, which have only very recently broken down in Catholic circles, leaving a huge and uncomfortable void.

Since the time of Augustine of Hippo, and probably much before that, catechists have been wrestling with the question as to what constitutes the characteristic morality of Christians and what therefore should be included in a Christian cate-chesis. It is extremely difficult to give a sensible answer to this question. Scripture scholars have been at pains to point out that Jesus did not teach a content for morality that was differ-ent from the already existing teaching of the rabbis but that he gave it the perspective of a far greater urgency and a cer-tain ruthless simplicity. In the mid-second century, in the document known as the *Didaché*, we find evidence that the Christian catechesis in fact presented as its moral teaching what Israel taught its proselytes. Augustine, in response to his catechists, gave the answer that probably is still the correct answer today. The catechumen must be initiated into the mo-rality spelled out in the Sinai code and summarized slogan-style in the Ten Commandments. Only after that should he be introduced to the New Testament understanding, which reduces all that went before to the simplest dimensions of love of God and love of neighbor.

This answer probably still stands, but it begs the question. If there is a Christian perspective in morality, it consists evidently of this ruthless reduction of everything to the total—passionate—love of God and of fellowmen. But the same can be said, of course, of the more sensitive and subtle traditions within Judaism before and since the time of Jesus. Moreover, this emphasis on a love commandment is curiously unhelpful if left dangling in the air, timelessly, without father or mother or posterity. To command love is to command creative response to need and creative response to gift. But the creative response is precisely what cannot be spelled out or legislated. To command love, therefore, is to command what can be done only through the understanding that comes from the critique of praxis. The New Testament, in fact, shows the command of love addressed principally to the community as such. If creative breakthroughs into the radically new are possible, it is because Jesus himself is the beginning and because the community of believers links us to that beginning. It is in the unity and solidarity of that community endeavor that we are able to learn what kinds of responses are called forth by love.

In fact, the community throughout the ages has been keenly aware of this and we have built up a great heritage of wisdom in relation to moral values and priorities. This heritage does not consist of final answers to all questions. It consists of a great deal of experience of trying to live by the vision of Jesus Christ, a great deal of reflection on what was self-authenticating and what proved self-defeating in that experience, and frequent attempts to draw some kind of normative guide for future action. It includes, for instance, the natural law concept, which rests on the important contention that morality is not arbitrary but rests on the very being of things, on reality itself, and consists of the wisdom that God shares with men through their experience and their reason. It is founded on the further conviction that morality is therefore basically one for all men and that all can participate in the common search for right conduct.

The Catholic heritage of wisdom concerning moral values and priorities also contains reflection on praxis that results in some very specific convictions, for example, about the protection of human life and the right of all to the natural resources of the earth. It is right that today's religious educators should be wary of facile and prefabricated answers to complex and new questions; they should be uncomfortable with the suggestion that the proper way to deal with moral issues is to ask Rome for a ruling on the matter. But it is most unfortunate that there is also a tendency to speak as though any opinion were as good as any other, as though the Catholic community and its tradition have nothing to offer towards a solution. This is simply untrue. What we have to offer is the ongoing critique of praxis in which these questions are not being asked for the first time and are not being asked in a chaotic or unfocused context. They are being asked in the context of some previous answers that "did not work" and of some that did.

We do not have a computer to turn out answers to practical questions about particular moral situations and decisions. We do have as a community some well-matured habits of reflection, judgment, and decision and some well-tested general patterns of priorities and values. These we hold on trust from generations who lived in this tradition before us, and we must pass them along to the generations that come after us. They are the community's support in the forming of a vigorous, critical, and creative conscience—that is, a habit of judging what is right to do in particular moments and situations that tends to be vigorous, critical, and creative. Nothing that we hand on is a substitute for these creative, personal judgments and decisions either in public or in private life. Yet neither can these judgments and decisions be made out of nothing. They are made out of values and perceptions shaped by each man or woman on the basis of what has been offered to this person by environment and by formal and informal education. If the environment is pluralistic and permissive, offering little rootedness in the wisdom of past generations, and if education does not supply this either, the individual has very little to work with in the shaping of his habits of moral judgment and decision.

NOTES

What is described in this chapter must be found in living dialogue rather than in a textbook. The closest to it that can be done by books is being attempted in the so-called "liberation theology," e.g. *A Theology of Liberation,* by Gustavo Gutierrez (Orbis Books, Maryknoll, 1973).

For the historical formation of the creeds, see my book *The Christian Creeds: a Faith to Live By* (Pflaum, 1973) and the bibliography given at the ends of the chapters for more depth.

CHAPTER 7:
THE COMMUNITY STRUCTURES ITSELF

There seems to be a feeling among many religious educators and other zealous Catholics that the present crisis of understanding and confidence could be surmounted well enough if it were not for the structure of the Church. This attitude, of course, is not peculiar to the Catholic situation nor to religious concerns. It is a contemporary feeling about many situations. It is not necessarily a good omen or bad, but it ought to be understood properly and put into perspective.

Structure happens wherever there is life. When we speak of structure in relation to people, we mean predictable patterns of behavior. Language is a structure. Sleeping at night is a structure. Thumbing a ride or hailing a taxi is a structure. We could not do anything creative or personal without the support of structures. But it is a common human experience that individuals and societies often fail to do the creative because they allow structures to form a horizon for all that is seen as the real rather than to use them as scaffolding to support new endeavors. At any time, there are people who fall into this pattern in all or most phases of their lives, and there are at least a few who chafe at this pattern because they have discerned what is happening. At a time of particularly rapid change, however, there are moments when the existing structures are so obviously inadequate to a new challenge that almost everybody is chafing at the structures and that the very idea of structure begins to have a predominantly negative value to many persons. This does not necessarily mean that change swiftly follows. Social structures can become so complex that, even when almost everyone within a structure is dissatisfied with it, no one is really able to imagine the alternates or to plan and execute the dismantling or modification of the existing inadequate structure. There may be frustration and discontent for a long time. If it is not examined and handled intelligently, there can be a great deal of energy lost in fighting false enemies.

Several categories of structure appear to be a problem to Catholics today on a wide scale. Prominent among them is the hierarchic structure of the clergy. Immediately linked with this structure are Canon Law and the control of membership rules of the community. Also linked with it is the structure of the community's coming together in public worship, connected with which is the question considered in the last chapter, namely its catechesis: what is taught within the community as creed and code.

Many Catholics, perhaps a steadily increasing number, are finding these structures very oppressive today. This must be due, at least in part, to the rapidity of change in experience and perception in the world in general and in the Catholic community, and this leaves a culture gap that is difficult to bridge. It may also be due, however, to a continuing false pattern of expectations. There is still a tendency among Catholics today to expect too much from the structures, to expect what structures are never capable of yielding, to expect the structures to beget life. Structures cannot beget life, though life structures itself. An organization cannot make community though community organizes itself. Hierarchic structures do not prophesy, though prophets may influence and build up hierarchic structures. Laws do not anticipate public conscience and needs, but public conscience and needs anticipate and create laws. Rubrics do not guarantee that a community is truly praying as one; but when a community prays as one, somehow or other rubrics always shape up.

The present disenchantment with structures, especially with the hierarchic structure of the clergy, seems to be connected intimately with an attitude in which "the Church" almost always means the clergy, or more particularly, the higher clergy, perhaps quite specifically the Roman Curia (often thought of simplistically as though its every utterance came straight from the person of the Pope). In this case, every reflection concerning what the Church ought to do becomes a wish rather than a hope, a demand on others rather than an engagement of one's own resources, perhaps recrimination rather than a constructive move for change.

Respect for tradition and community and for the practical, common-sense reality of the Church is integral to the Catholic heritage. If we do not hand that over to those who come after us, we have betrayed the trust. But enslavement to structure or to particular structures, commonplace as it may be in our history through the ages, must be seen as abuse and deviation from the quest for the Reign of God. The correct differentiation between the two is a difficult and delicate task of discernment. It should astonish no one that there is so little agreement over it. The religious educator today must surely acknowledge, for instance, the head-on clash between the Roman Curia and some of the most distinguished theologians of our time over the question of papal infallibility. Nor can he hide the confusion over authority in matters of morality following in the wake of the birth-control controversy and the encyclical *Humanae vitae*. It is clearly of the utmost importance in the handing on of the Catholic heritage to deal with these issues in a way that enables individuals and the community to keep their balance and to pursue the objective of the whole enterprise of Church, namely the redemption of the world into the Reign of God.

The most fundamental task in this quest seems to be the recapturing of the awareness that we—the whole community, the laity—*are* the Church, in an active and not only in a passive sense. The present structures are what the community over the ages has made them and what the community of the present maintains. All leadership operates in complex patterns. The community chooses its leaders directly or indirectly, obviously or subtly; and it imposes on them patterns of expectation. In turn, the leaders exercise choice, more or less, as to how to respond to those expectations; and they in turn shape the community. Everyone shares the responsibility for the kind of leadership the community has and for the way the community shapes itself. Because it is axiomatic in Catholicism that the support of the community makes a difference and that the traditions built by the community's experience support the Christian quest, this responsibility has to be taken very seriously.

We learn from our history though we might arrive at the same conclusion simply from reflection—that there basically are two different types of leadership in the Church. There is the leading of the community in a formal and organized way in worship and in any type of corporate action. This leadership mainly functions to consolidate what has been achieved, to preserve the heritage from the past, to coordinate so that many can do things together, to harmonize conflicts, and so forth. A quite different leadership is one that sparks new insights, makes a new breakthrough in Christian action in the world, challenges the accepted understanding. Such a leadership cannot assume the following of the whole people or even of a substantial number. Such leadership always is controversial and is bound to appear as divisive. Such leadership anticipates the history of the community rather than consolidates what already has passed. These two types of leadership are those of the hierarch and of the prophet. We cannot expect our bishops and popes to be prophets. Only under the rarest circumstances, in times of bitter persecution, when the community itself has become a controversial minority challenging the status quo in its society, can the two roles conceivably be combined. They demand mutually exclusive attitudes to the community as present, concrete reality. To ask our bishops and popes to be prophets is to basically fail in our own vocation. We need prophets in every time and place and situation, but they must come from the people by a different route than that by which the hierarchy comes from the people.

This would seem to be of import for religious education. It is necessary to build the vision and expectation of the community so that the prophet does not scandalize when he prophesies but also so that the hierarchy does not scandalize when it does not prophesy. It is necessary to build the vision and expectation of the community so that individuals within it may be alert to receive the gift of prophecy, which cannot be done when there is a sense of antagonism to hierarchy or hierarchic structure.

Much the same might be said concerning Church legislation and the regulation of public worship and the celebration of the sacraments. These are activities that the Church does corporately. Regulation makes it possible to do them corporately. Regulation will always tend to lag behind the cultural changes in the community's language, emotional tonality, symbols, and sense of the sacred. If we expect the regulations to anticipate our cultural changes, we simply are not responding to our own vocation within the community to shape its prayer and sensitivity to God revealing himself. Yet true creativity in prayer is not really possible without a respectful discipleship within the tradition with its established prayer patterns. There is no limit to creative shaping of one's own style of personal prayer. But creative shaping of new styles of communal prayer cannot assume the agreement of the majority; it necessarily will appeal to a few at least at the beginning, and it almost necessarily will be seen as divisive. That they are seen as divisive is not in itself a condemnation of pentecostal groups, Bible meditation groups, spontaneous prayer groups, and the like. But it does mean that it is not new forms that unite the community but the classic and agreed forms of prayer, which have shaped up so slowly that they will never seem up-to-date, and which must serve such a variety of societies and cultures that they will seldom appear as most immediately relevant to a particular group. Patience with this compromise seems to be one of the key elements of Catholicism, and it is one that is rather important to pass on.

Again, in this case, a grasp of our own history makes it much simpler to attain the necessary breadth and depth of vision to deal with practical issues in a constructive and tolerant way that allows for the greatest development. It is however, more than an intellectual enterprise. There is a question of one's personal order of urgency and importance. A tolerant and sensible approach to the problems of structure becomes much easier for any Catholic once he realizes that the Church is first and foremost a movement of the followers of Jesus to bring about the redemption of the world into the Reign of God. Such a movement is like the proverbial iceberg that is nine-tenths submerged under the water. The overwhelming mass of redemptive activity by Catholics is not under hierarchic or legislative supervision at all, but it is in the free-flowing stream of the community's life lived in response to the situation in the world. Most of the activity that is Church is not socially very visible. It is true that the community essentially constitutes itself by gathering around the Eucharist; but the essential action is the gathering together to be personally present at the redemptive death of Jesus, bringing to it one's life experience and taking from it some personal assimilation of the mind and heart of Christ and the unity and support of a community that is on the same quest. The inner reality of the action is not controlled at all by rubrics.

An important part of passing on the heritage is to give a vital experience and explanation of the ritual of public worship. This certainly means some understanding of the history or development of the rites, of the stories from which their symbolism was constructed, and of the theology that has been elaborated out of that symbolism. It may be well to approach this understanding through other experiences whose ritual and symbolism are drawn from contemporary life. But there really is no way to avoid experience and explanation in depth of the classic patterns of liturgical worship and yet pass along the Catholic heritage.

On the other hand, it is possible to make the same mistake with the liturgy that has so commonly been made with the creeds. As central as the liturgy is to the Catholic heritage, it does not exist for its own sake, and it does not have any autonomous efficacy. It exists to promote the unity and charity and clarity of vision within the Church community that will enable that community to bring about in Christ the redemption of the world into the Reign of God. The Church does not exist for the sake of the Church but for the sake of the Reign of God yet to be established among men. The liturgy does not exist for the sake of beautiful ritual, a sense of serenity or uplift, or a swinging experience of togetherness but for the sake of moving men into so living as to bring about the Reign of God in the world. Hierarchy does not exist for the sake of the structure nor ordained ministry for the sake of the clergy. Each exists for the sake of the unity and continuity of the

Church so that it can devote itself to its central task, which is not "churchy" in any sense at all.

This realization appears to be important for the solution of our present dilemma with structures of all types. These structures are frequently the vehicle for what we are handing on in the tradition, and they must be respected as such under pain of losing the substance of the tradition somewhere along the line. But the structures are at all times relative to the goals and purposes they serve. They are judged from the perspective of the future that is yet a hope, not from the perspective of the past. Moreover, the structures are not entities but action, the action of the community organizing itself. We are that community, but we are not the whole of the community. The unity by which the whole can collaborate closely and share in common understanding and recollection and creative projections of the future—this unity is immensely important in terms of our goals as Church.

In the process of religious education, familiarity with the structures and their history and purpose must certainly be provided. Yet we must proceed in a way that permits each person in the Catholic community to come to this familiarity as one actively striving for the goals of the community, taking his own initiatives, with an eye on ultimate and immediate goals, and then discovering the structures that make possible the collaboration with others and the solidarity of the community. It is certainly necessary that the structures in which the life and tradition of the community are carried be introduced and recognized as human activities, not as magic. When they are seen as instrumental relationships and patterns of behavior, error and inadequacy are expected and tolerated and recognized as such so that they can be corrected. When the structures are seen as divinely guaranteed and autonomously subsisting entities, somehow expected to operate independently of the men whose action they are, we are in danger of naive credulity, superstitious practices, impossible expectations, culminating either in downright refusal to accept the truth or in a desperate sense of having been betrayed. Either way, all the energy and human resources necessary for personal and creative involvement in the task of the redemption of the world are deflected into wearying and quite fruitless busyness with the internal minutiae of the community.

Because they are professionals within the Church system, it is perhaps particularly crucial at this time that religious educators (including catechists, teachers, and preachers of all kinds) put their own house in order concerning their attitudes toward and understanding of the Church as institutional structure, including the hierarchy, the liturgy, and the various patterns of control. What is most surely handed on in the educational process is the educator's own attitude. It is communicated whether or not his techniques are good, his explanations clear, or the time propitious. Yet at this time, it is precisely the professional in the Church system who is most frequently and most profoundly ambivalent about the structures in which he operates. It is precisely the professional who frequently expresses the greatest sense of powerlessness within the system and the most strident impatience with human limitation and error and prejudice and lack of imagination reflected in the structures.

The professional, of course, suffers more from all of these, and he has better opportunities to experience at first hand the problems and limitations. Yet he also is more strategically placed to do something about them. If he feels powerless and assumes that nothing can be done, then indeed the machinery has been abandoned and is running out of control. The unpalatable truth is that everything is possible to those who are willing to pay the price for it and who are open to the possibility of discovering that their own judgments have been wrong. This basically is the message of the Cross, the central symbol of our whole tradition.

NOTES

Particularly helpful in relation to the subject matter of this chapter are the essays in *Readings in the Theology of the Church* edited by Edward Dirkswager (Prentice-Hall, 1968). In relation to the underlying theory, see also *The Dynamic Element in the Church* by Karl Rahner (Herder, 1964).

CONCLUSION:
WHAT HAVE WE TO HAND ON?

The thrust of the previous chapters has been that Catholic religious education is in crisis at present, not over the question as to how we are to hand on the Catholic heritage but over the more fundamental question as to what exactly is the heritage that we have to hand on to future generations. The crisis is one both of understanding and of confidence, but the latter is unwarranted because we have the resources to resolve the whole issue immediately.

The thesis of this book is very simple, though the implementation of it is obviously complex. At its most fundamental level, what we have to hand on is the experience of a promise that has totally transformed our perception of the world and of our life in it and the long experience of the community's response of faith and hope and action on the strength of that promise. At its most fundamental level, what we have to hand on to others is an experience, and it is the experience of a large community that has lived over many centuries. An experience is handed on only when newcomers are included in the same event, not when they are told about it. Yet the telling may be necessary to actualize or to interpret the experience.

This experience of the community has been expressed and may be apprehended in several dimensions. In its broadest sweep, it is the quest for the Reign of God among men, pursued in the light of Jesus as the Christ. We are dealing with 20 centuries of efforts to better the life of mankind on the basis of the possibilities given in Jesus Christ.

These efforts can be understood and explained in the terms that the community has chosen as its classic formulations. These include, first and foremost, the documents collected in the Christian Bible. The meaning of these documents for Christians is not only what was intended by the original authors but what was intended in the selection of these documents for the canon of Scripture and was developed from the themes of various documents in the Bible collection and what became the understanding of the Church community as it meditated and tried to live the message of these documents in the light of its whole experience in Christ.

The classic formulations also include the lives that have been canonized as saintly and exemplary when the community has reflected upon them in retrospect, and the traditions of spirituality and of merciful and charitable works that have been given some sort of official recognition. These are the fruits of the community's discernment of what is focused most clearly on the coming Reign of God in its own experience.

Beyond this awareness, the classic formulations include more abstract or general fruits of the critique of the community's praxis in the form of creedal statements and definitions that provide the horizon for the interpretation of reality. They also include an ongoing process of describing the moral code and the cult of the community—a process of describing that also becomes prescribing. Such definitions are never the beginning of understanding or explaining, but rather the summary of what has already been understood or explained.

Finally, the classic formulations include the ways in which the community has structured itself for worship, for unity and continuity, for a discipline of membership rules. Such structure consists of the predictable patterns of behavior of the members of the community, and it has no existence other than in their actions and expectations. It suffers all the limitations of the persons whose behavior constitutes the structure. It is not the life stream of the tradition, but it is the channel through which the life stream flows. It exists entirely for the sake of the task of the Church in the world, and it must be shaped constantly to that task.

These are the elements of the Catholic heritage. These are the subject matter for tradition, the work of handing on the heritage. Religious education is that work become self-conscious, and it must be concerned seriously with these elements. Those who are religious educators must grasp them in as much depth and breadth as they can, remembering that all is judged with reference to the coming Reign of God, and the Reign of God is seen by Christians in terms of the possibilities glimpsed in Jesus Christ.